The 9 Super Simple Steps to
Entrepreneurial
Success

The **9** Super Simple Steps to
Entrepreneurial
Success

Martin J. Grunder Jr.

BETTERWAY BOOKS
CINCINNATI, OHIO

The Nine Super Simple Steps to Entrepreneurial Success. Copyright © by Martin J. Grunder Jr. Manufactured in the United States of America. All rights reserved. No part of this book may be reproduced in any form or by any electronic or mechanical means including information storage and retrieval systems without permission in writing from the publisher, except by a reviewer, who may quote brief passages in a review. Published by Betterway Books, an imprint of F&W Publications, Inc., 4700 East Galbraith Road, Cincinnati, OH 45236. (800) 289-0963. Second edition.

Visit our Web site at www.writersdigest.com for information on more resources for writers.

To receive a free weekly E-mail newsletter delivering tips and updates about writing and about Writer's Digest products, register directly at our Web site at http://newsletters.fwpublications.com.

07   06   05 04 03   5 4 3 2 1

Library of Congress Cataloging-in-Publication Data

Grunder, Martin J., 1968-
   The 9 super simple steps to entrepreneurial success / by Marty
Grunder.-- 2nd ed.
    p. cm.
   ISBN 1-55870-658-5 (pbk. : alk. paper)
    1. Entrepreneurship. 2. New business enterprises. 3. Success in
business. I. Title: Nine super simple steps to entrepreneurial success.
II. Title.

   HB615.G78   2003
   658.02'2—dc21

                      2003000714
                      CIP

Editor: Jerry Jackson Jr.
Production Coordinator: Michelle Ruberg
Cover design: Stanard Design Partners
Interior design: Dana Boll

iv

Dedicated to Dad
— You didn't get to read this book,
but you sure helped me write it!

Acknowledgments

Writing a book is a lot more work than people probably realize. It requires a lot of people to get something like this book done. I'd like to thank those people. First of all my wife Lisa and my kids, Emily, Kathleen, Lily, and Grant. They have supported me in the many late nights and weekends I spent working on this book and inspire me to continue to chase my dreams. I'd also like to thank my mom who has always encouraged and supported my entrepreneurial endeavors. She is an inspiration to me. A few more folks to thank are the great team of people I work with at Grunder Landscaping and The Winner's Circle, especially my partner Dave Rado and Nancy Ericson, my assistant. Nancy spent hours working on the rough drafts of this book and she is simply terrific. Finally, I'd like to recognize the many entrepreneurs around the U.S. and Canada who have let me help them chase their dreams. Dreaming is what our great country is all about. Now . . . let's get to work helping you with your dream.

About the Author

Marty Grunder

Born in 1968, Marty Grunder is the founder and president of Grunder Landscaping Company in Dayton, Ohio. Grunder Landscaping was started in 1983 with a $25 mower bought at a garage sale as a way to make money for college. By the time he was a senior at the University of Dayton, Marty's company grossed over $300,000 and his story appeared in *The New York Times.* Today Grunder Landscaping employs forty-plus professionals and enjoys annual sales of more than 3 million dollars. Grunder Landscaping has won more than thirty local and national awards for their entrepreneurial efforts. Marty is a two-time Young Entrepreneur of the Year for the State of Ohio and also was awarded Young Entrepreneur of the Year for the entire Midwest by the Small Business Administration. And he was one of ten finalists for the Young Entrepreneur of the Year Award for the entire United States. In 2001, Marty was awarded the Ernst & Young Entrepreneur of the Year Award for Dayton/Miami Valley.

In 1995 Marty formed Marty Grunder! Inc., a business consulting company offering entrepreneurs help with marketing, management, and motivation. A highly sought after professional speaker, teacher, and authority on success, Marty has spoken all over the U.S. and Canada. Marty has given his high-energy, humorous talks to thousands of people, young and old, inspiring them to pursue their dreams.

He lives in Centerville, Ohio, with his wife Lisa, three daughters Emily, Kathleen, and Lillian, and son Grant.

Table of Contents

Introduction

Why is success seemingly so easy for some and so elusive for others? Are some people just born to be successful? Is it education that makes someone successful? What about the guy next door? You've noticed he is a very successful entrepreneur, and you think you could be too, but how? How does he do it? Then there's that thirty-year-old former nurse you know who started her own business and is now not just happy but wealthy. How did she do that? How can you do it? How is it people and even entire families move here from far-away places like India, Lebanon, China, or Japan and become wildly successful? Is there some mysterious trait all these people share, or are they just lucky? *The Nine Super Simple Steps to Entrepreneurial Success* will answer those questions and unlock the secret to your success. Whether you are twelve, thirty, forty-five, sixty, or eighty, an aspiring entrepreneur or a struggling entrepreneur, this book will show you how to achieve entrepreneurial success.

As you read my book, you'll find out how Grunder Landscaping Company grew from a two-person after-school lawn mowing operation (just like the one you might have had once, or have now) to a national award-winning multimillion-dollar success. As the company was growing, I relentlessly studied other successful people and companies and found similarities amongst all of them. All of the successful people I studied loved their work (**had a passion for it**). These people were very **goal** oriented. Many of them learned how to be successful on someone else's payroll (**got paid to learn**). They had a core group of friends and mentors (**surrounded themselves with winners**) who were very successful. They had a tremendous amount of confidence in themselves (**believed in themselves**). They weren't afraid to **ask questions**—why things happened the way that they did. They **focused** on a niche. They did things a little bit differently, they operated in a way that was contrary to the norm, and they weren't afraid to break the rules. And, last but not least, the successful people I studied all **worked very, very, very hard**. Throughout the book you will find "reality checks." I felt that these would help you realize everything isn't always perfect. These quick and to-the-point paragraphs will help you avoid pitfalls many fall into.

And that's the story of *The Nine Super Simple Steps to Entrepreneurial Success*. This book is a blueprint for your entrepreneurial success. I have had many successful people read this book prior to its release. Some, like my millionaire entrepreneurial friend Dr. Michael Ervin, said that in retrospect the nine steps were exactly what he used to become successful. Others have used the steps to bring their dreams to life and have achieved success by following them. I hope you enjoy the book. I would love to hear your comments about it, and I am always available to help grow you and your business at (937) 847-9944, or visit my company at www.martygrunder.com. Enjoy.

chapter one

Entrepreneurship— the Path to Success

Hopefully, you purchased this book (or were given it as a gift) because you want to run your own business. Or maybe you are already an entrepreneur and want to do better. As you know, entrepreneurship is hot, really hot. But actually it's been hot for about two hundred years, and I don't see it slowing down . . . EVER! In a recent Gallup poll nearly seven out of ten high school students said they wanted to start and run their own business. The students said they wanted to do this because they wanted to be their own boss. Who doesn't want to be their own boss? Is this your dream?

Many people, young and old, dream of running their own business. There's something very exciting about seeing your dream take shape and supporting yourself and your family on your own.

Millions of people today control their own destiny running all kinds of businesses. Many become entrepreneurs by being part of successful multi-level marketing groups like Amway, Nutrition for Life, Excel Communications, Longaberger Baskets, USANA, and Nikken. Countless others run contracting companies, service companies, retail establishments, and manufacturing plants. Other people are creating incredible, successful organizations with the invention of the Internet. Proof is in the amazing stories of com-

1

panies like Amazon.com, EMC, Cisco, Excite, Yahoo, and Ebay, a lot of these run by very young people. And then there are firms like the well-known Wal-Mart and Home Depot, and many not-so-well-known firms started by people when they were fifty or older. If you ever doubt the popularity of entrepreneurship, just drive through any downtown, and you'll see entrepreneurial endeavors everywhere. Even your doctor may have an entrepreneurial mind. Physicians are finding creative ways to do business. Eye doctors and chiropractors are two current examples of physicians using imagination and business savvy to succeed as entrepreneurs.

Each year an estimated five million Americans start their own business. It's easy to understand why. It's not very much fun nor is it comforting to know that the company you work for at any time may downsize and leave you without a job. That happens. I've seen huge corporations let people go for all kinds of reasons. I've had clients of our landscaping company get transferred because a consultant hired by their employer decided it would be better to have a particular operation in another city to "improve efficiency." I even know of one rather large corporation that moved corporate offices to Baltimore from the Midwest because that's where the CEO was originally from. As a lifelong entrepreneur, I can't imagine having someone else control my future like that. It is far more likely that the company you are employed by will fire, lay off, or sever your employment with them than it would be for all your clients of your own business to fire you. In fact, you may be reading this book because you are sick of this "control" too and want to control your own destiny! I want to inspire you to be a successful entrepreneur, and teach you how.

You Have to Do More Than Dream

Do you want to be the top salesperson in your multi-level marketing group? Do you want to own your own car repair shop? Is a restaurant your dream? Or do you want to start a landscaping company? There's nothing wrong with dreaming; it keeps many of us going. But you have to do more than dream.

Whatever you want to do, you can be successful at it, but to be a successful entrepreneur, you have to have a map. You need to know where you're going and how to get there. No one wakes up on Saturday and says to their family, "Surprise! Wake up! We're going on vacation. Everybody get in the car." And then proceeds to drive aimlessly across the country. You always plan your vacation. Some people plan their vacations months in advance and even down to the hour. Why? We do this to save time and money, eliminate frustration, and to guarantee a good time. Few people, unfortunately, plan their lives and their businesses with the same care. They never take time to think about who they are, what they want to do, and how they're going to get there. Until you take the time to do this, you never will realize your full potential. As the often-used adage goes, "Fail to plan, plan to fail."

This book will provide sound, simple advice and examples as well as inspiration for you to plan your dream of being an entrepreneur. You won't need a business degree from Harvard to understand it. The nine steps outlined here are from the exact blueprint I used to start and build one of the most successful landscape companies in the U.S. My nine steps take you from the inception to the maturity of your business.

Many people I work with at my consulting company, Marty Grunder! Inc., don't realize how many talents and opportunities for

3

entrepreneurship they have until I force them to list all their past jobs, skills, passions, and hobbies. Once they see all that they really have the ability to do, they are able to begin the process of living their entrepreneurial dream. I hope to help bring out the talents you have, too, but I want to stress that word "process." Success is a process. It does not come overnight. It comes from a constant commitment to a goal over a long period of time. (I often tell people Grunder Landscaping Company is an eighteen-year overnight success story!) Those who realize this, regardless of their age, don't give up when problems or obstacles come between them and their goal. They look at obstacles as merely learning experiences. In fact, successful people become so focused on their goal, nothing can stop them.

In my own entrepreneurial experience and my years of research, I have found most successful people will vocalize their goals to anyone who will listen. I do this to help motivate myself. Successful people have a burning, competitive desire. When they say they're going to do something, they do it. They can't imagine not achieving a goal, so they tell anyone who will listen what their goal is. That way, when times get tough, and they feel like giving up, they say to themselves, "I can't quit. I told all those people what I was going to do, and I'm sure not going to tell them I quit and couldn't do it." A real-life example of this is the book you are reading right now. In writing this book, I used my nine steps. After attending a seminar for speakers and authors, I conceived the idea of writing *The Nine Super Simple Steps to Entrepreneurial Success*. I felt there was a real need for a book like this—a down-to-earth, easy-to-understand approach to realizing the entrepreneurial dream.

A few months later, I had a deal with a publisher to produce the book. So, off I went writing and telling everyone to watch out for my new book. I even ended all my e-mails by saying, "Watch out for my new book 'The Nine Super Simple Steps to Entrepreneurial Success,' available soon." Six months later, I said, "There's no way I can do this." I was writing every available moment,

"IT MAY BE THAT
THOSE WHO DO MOST,
DREAM MOST."

—Stephen Leacock, economist and humorist

working eighty hours a week at a very successful, growing company; and trying to be a father, husband, son, brother, and friend. Trying to be everything at once is tough. Many days, I didn't feel like writing. Some days, I even felt like quitting. And I had my share of doubts. Would the book sell? Would readers like it? Would I get it done by my deadline? But every time I started to feel like quitting, I quickly remembered all the people I'd told I was going to have a new book out, and I went right back to work. And therein lies a lesson that weaves through this whole book—persistence! Reading this book will take some time and commitment on your part. I encourage you, as you read this book, to take notes, to highlight pages and bend them over. And to read it a couple of times. Have the most significant people in your life read this book, too. That way they can help you reach your goal! But do it, don't stop here. Don't read one-half of it and put it down. Read the whole book. I read a study once that said only seventeen percent of the books consumers buy are ever read. Make this book part of the seventeen percent. I promise you it will be one of the best investments you ever make, if not the best one. Reading and finishing this book will be an accomplishment for you to build on. I've known a lot of people who spend hours talking about what they're going to do and seconds actually doing anything about it. If you're one of those talkers, you could change into a doer if you finish this book.

The nine steps one needs to take to be successful are easy to understand. However, I don't want to mislead you—the work you will have to put forth to be successful will not be easy. There is no magical potion one can put together and, "Presto," be successful. But this book will show and tell you what you can do to make your dream a reality.

I hope you enjoy reading it as much as I did writing it. Look at me as a real, normal person who is successful. Start looking at yourself as a successful person, and you're halfway there.

chapter two

Pick a Passion

"I'd rather be awful at something I love than great at
something I hate."

—George Burns

Growing up on a miniature farm, surrounded by real farms, in southern Ohio, it was second nature for me to operate tractors, work hard, and be outside. We had a lot of grass to cut and by age seven, I could proficiently operate all lawn mowing equipment. As you can imagine, anything that has an engine and you can drive is the ultimate toy for a young man. For me, a tractor was my car. I loved to cut grass. It was my passion.

This passion strangely enough was fueled by baseball. I watched a lot of baseball on TV growing up. My dad got me hooked as we spent hours watching games. Games broadcast from the old Candlestick Park in California, home of the San Francisco Giants, always caught my eye. The mowing lines in the field were flawless. You could see what pride and attention to detail the grounds crew had. I looked at the lush green manicured field and dreamt of mowing lawns that would look like that when I was done.

To me cutting grass enabled me to be creative. I would take my time mowing my parents' lawn. In fact, many times I took a job that should have taken three hours and turned it into a six-hour job because I wanted our yard to look like Candlestick Park. I remember my mom telling me, when I was nine years old, that "The lawn looks much better now that you're mowing it instead of your father." Talk about positive reinforcement! My mom always knew how to make me feel good about myself. (She still does today.) I enjoyed mowing lawns so much I began to wonder if people would pay me to create a little art in their yards, pay me to smell the pleasing (to me) aroma of fresh cut grass, and pay me to drive my tractor around their yard. Pro baseball players get paid to have fun; I concluded that I should too.

Today, though I own a landscaping company, I still often cut my own lawn for all the above reasons. My wife and neighbors kid me about it, but the truth is, I find it very therapeutic. It is one of my passions. And I have taken that passion several steps further. Today Grunder Landscaping Company is a multimillion-dollar operation operating out of a world-class facility situated on sixteen acres along Interstate 75 thirteen miles south of Dayton, Ohio. Stop by and see us sometime. I'll personally show you the power of a passion. Grunder Landscaping Company installs creative landscaping, water gardens, night lighting, paver driveways, patios and walks, and we offer maintenance services for everything we install. Visit us at www.grunderlandscaping.com. We have won more than thirty local and national awards for our efforts. I was twice named Young Entrepreneur of the Year for the state of Ohio by the Small Business Administration and once named Young Entrepreneur of the Year for the entire Midwest by the Small Business Administration. In 2001 I was named Entrepreneur of the Year by Ernst & Young in the service category in Dayton, Ohio. Even though we are a much bigger company today than when I started Grunder Landscaping many years ago, passion still drives us.

My passion has also opened up other doors. Today I spend much of my time traveling through the U.S. giving motivational talks, advising other entrepreneurs on how to market and manage, and motivating them to new heights. But I still love landscaping and serve as CEO of Grunder Landscaping Company and continue to design and sell creative landscaping as my time allows. We often ask our clients why they do business with us. Many comment, "We chose Grunder Landscaping Company because of your enthusiasm for our project." Never forget that word "enthusiasm." It can be the difference between success and failure.

As you can guess, landscaping is a very competitive business. How has Grunder Landscaping Company reached the top of our profession in a relatively short amount of time? I insist my staff be chock full of people who love landscaping and making clients happy. We do not hire laid-back people to sell our landscaping services. My entire management team gardens in their spare time, some more than others, but they all do it. One of the main reasons we've been able to be so successful is our enthusiasm. Employees buy into enthusiasm and love to show their best in a culture full of passion. My company is a very upbeat place, because people like rallying around a cause.

Clients and customers buy enthusiasm and passion too. Money is a very important thing to most. Many only have so much and guard it closely. They think about purchases before they make them. The average job Grunder Landscaping Company does is around $5,000. We also regularly do jobs over $30,000 and have done several jobs over $100,000. Seventy-five percent of our work is residential landscaping, and rarely are we the lowest bid on the table so we have to do an excellent job of convincing prospects that it is worth spending more money to hire us. We have plenty of proof we present—pictures of completed projects and testimonials from other happy clients, but most importantly, we demonstrate passion for our work. People buy from people who show passion for their work. People buy from Grunder Landscaping Company because they see our passion and believe that we'll do a great job; they trust us and sense our pride in our work.

You too must pick a passion to be successful and, if George Burns, at ninety plus, realized this, you can, at your age, do it too. My passion was working outside. Cutting grass was fun. A lot of fun in fact. I wasn't, as a youngster, driven by money. I was driven by my passion for cutting grass. It just so happened that I was making money too, and that's the way it should be. You're having fun and, oh, by the way, making money.

To be the very best you can be at a particular job, to achieve a goal and to be successful, you must love what you are doing. The love or passion we have for the work itself or the subsequent goal that can be seen in the distance makes the work easy. Jimmy Carter, the 39th President of the United States, said it well in an interview I read once in *Investors Business Daily*. He said, "If you have a task to perform and are vitally interested in it, excited and challenged by it, then you will exert maximum energy. In the excitement, the pain and fatigue dissipate and the exuberance of what you hope to achieve overcomes the wariness." I have found what President Carter said to be true.

I have two different companies. The first is Grunder Landscaping Company, the company I started in 1983 with a $25 lawn mower bought at a garage sale. Today the company has forty employees and annual sales of more than 3 million in a small market. My other company is Marty Grunder! Inc. At Marty Grunder & Associates we help entrepreneurs and aspiring entrepreneurs with marketing, management, and motivation. We put on educational boot camps and design and produce products to help entrepreneurs grow their bank accounts. I also do motivational and educational speaking all over the U.S. and Canada. You must know by now that I love my jobs, and it is no problem to get up every morning and go to work. Whether I am at home in Dayton, Ohio, working at Grunder Landscaping or in Los Angeles, California, pursuing my other passion, speaking to a group of aspiring entrepreneurs, I love my work. It is my passion and so easy for me to excel at.

There are a lot of things I could do. For example, I know that I could be a very good residential real estate salesman if I wanted to, and, seemingly, there is a lot to like about being one. The hours are flexible, the commissions can be good, and you're helping families find new homes. However, I do not like working Sundays, a must in residential real estate. I also don't like paperwork, and I'm not sure I'd like telling someone that somebody doesn't like their house and doesn't want to buy it. For those reasons, residential real estate is not something I like. It is not my passion. And how could I be good at it if I don't love it? Plain and simple, if you do not love the line of work you're in, you will become bored, complacent, and ineffective. You may become so miserable that your family and friends don't want to be around you much. The expression "whistle while you work" is the test. Do you whistle while you work? If you don't, quit and find something that you love. Dr. Nate Booth is an excellent example of this.

Dr. Nate Booth graduated from dental school at the University of Nebraska in 1971. He was in private practice for over eight years. And he hated it. Realizing dentistry was not his passion, Dr. Booth went back to school and earned a master's degree in counseling in 1983. He then began a speaking career and for more than seventeen years now Dr. Booth (www.natebooth.com) has motivated thousands of people to be the best they can be.

Dr. Booth quit dentistry because he realized it wasn't his passion. Money was not an issue, as dentists are well paid. Being happy was important. Give him immense credit for pursuing his passion of helping people and having the guts to do this at age thirty-five with a family to support. This passion has turned into a very lucrative business. He has written two books, *Thriving on Change: The Art of Using Change to Your Advantage* and *The Diamond Touch: How to Get What You Want by Giving People What They Uniquely Desire*, and he produces a newsletter. I recommend these books, by the way. A highly regarded speaker, Dr. Booth's passion is clearly visible in each and every one of his talks. From a business standpoint Nate Booth has a million-dollar business with only two employees! He's a great person too. When I initially met him at a conference, he spent three hours with me helping me with my own career. To this day he serves as an inspiration and mentor to me.

Money Only Motivates So Far

I was discussing pursuing a passion with a friend of mine once, and he shared a story with me. My friend's college roommate was studying pre-med at the time, and doing very well. He thought he wanted to be a doctor and often spoke of how much money doctors made. As part of one of his classes in his junior year at college, he went to a hospital to observe a surgery. A young man was getting his knee ligament repaired from an injury that occurred in a collegiate soccer game. As he watched the surgeon make the incision for the surgery, the pre-med student fainted, and on the way down, hit his head on a metal surgical tray. He cut his head so badly it required forty stitches. The doctor administered these stitches, and the young student went home.

That weekend while recovering from a huge headache, he decided to change his major to pre-law, and today he's a successful attorney in Cleveland, Ohio. He realized that even though he was fascinated by medicine and would like to make the money good doctors can make, he was afraid of blood and really did not like the hours a physician keeps. Medicine, in fact, was not his passion. His passions were helping people and being challenged. He found he could pursue these passions just as well in law school. Law became his passion. Today he is an extremely successful attorney and, oh, by the way, he is making money.

Keep in mind that money only motivates so far. The old saving "Money can't buy happiness" is true. If you're driven only by how much money you can make, you will never be happy. You must love your work. It has to be your passion. I challenge you to find a successful entrepreneur whose success cannot be directly attributed to his or her passion.

I always encourage college students to do a co-op or an internship in their major. This is a way of finding out if you really like a field, to find your passion or test what you think may be your passion. A co-op is when you actually get paid, while still in school, to do a job in the field you're majoring in. In an internship, typically, you do not get paid. But internships, too, can be very beneficial. Case in

13

point, a friend and client of my landscaping company, Dr. Kevin Paley, is a very successful entrepreneur/orthopedic surgeon in Dayton, Ohio. He did two years of free work in Los Angeles, California, under Dr. Frank Jobe, a legend in sports medicine. The knowledge he gained while treating members of the Los Angeles Dodgers and Los Angeles Lakers has enabled him to build a wildly successful sports medicine practice. His competitive advantages are the techniques he learned in that internship. You could say he

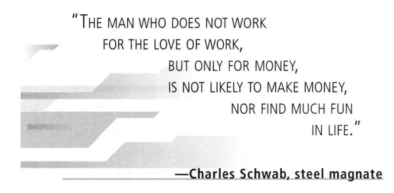

"THE MAN WHO DOES NOT WORK
FOR THE LOVE OF WORK,
BUT ONLY FOR MONEY,
IS NOT LIKELY TO MAKE MONEY,
NOR FIND MUCH FUN
IN LIFE."

—Charles Schwab, steel magnate

worked for free, but really he gained millions of dollars worth of ideas.

Consider also my father, Martin J. Grunder, Sr. Dad was not an entrepreneur, but his story proves my point. He enrolled at Seton Hall University in 1951 to pursue a degree in accounting. To put himself through school, Dad often worked summers for a construction company rough framing houses. He became very good at construction and began to really enjoy all aspects of constructing a house. The more classes he took in accounting, though, the less he liked it, and in 1953 Dad scrapped two years of work toward a degree in accounting and switched universities and majors. He enrolled in North Carolina State University's civil engineering school and graduated with a degree in civil engineering. Dad was then hired by the Ohio Department of Transportation where he worked successfully for more than thirty years, until he retired in 1997. It's a good thing Dad left accounting, because he probably wouldn't have made it.

I learned so much from my dad. We all learn a lot from our fathers. Dads have this magical power that inspires kids to chase their dreams. We believe what our fathers tell us, whether by words or actions. My dad passed away unexpectedly on November 1, 2000. I will never forget that sad day. But all my memories of my father are great. He was a very quiet man who never bragged about anything, but he was a good teacher. One of the best I've had. He silently taught me that you need to do what you enjoy. Thanks, Dad.

You could look at what my father did in two ways. You could say, "Why didn't he get more information on accounting before enrolling?" Heck, maybe you're even saying he wasted two years of his life. But what young person really understands the real world that well? Or you could praise my father for changing gears to pursue a passion. Dad initially chose accounting because his brother John said he'd like it. That was enough for my dad to make his decision and, as you may or may not know, it is perfectly normal to not know what you want to do with the rest of your life at any age. When we're young, especially, we're influenced greatly by our peers. We really don't know what the answers are to the questions, and we may not even know what the questions are! If something sounds okay, we don't have enough experience or courage to doubt it, so we say, "All right, I'll take it." It's okay to ask questions about a profession or line of work, folks, and we'll be talking a lot more about this in Chapter 8.

What is most important at this stage is to pick a passion. My dad may have erred initially by selecting accounting, but he found his passion by working a summer job he loved. Then he took his love for building several steps higher. Instead of houses, Dad engineered and oversaw the construction of several major state highway projects in Dayton and Cincinnati, Ohio. And that's the funny thing about picking a passion. It can literally be an overwhelming feeling when you find what you really want to do with the rest of your life. As we said earlier in the chapter, quoting President Carter, this passion makes you blind to all the obstacles. You see this goal at the end of a tunnel, and you don't see all the obstacles around it because of all the energy your passion gives you. Work is fun and slowly becomes a full-scale profession that you love.

Another person who comes to mind as being someone who certainly picked a passion and was able to pursue it well is Pete Rose. Pete Rose may have been a baseball player, but his story shows what passion can do! Pete Rose is the all-time hit leader in major league baseball with 4,256 hits. He was a tremendously determined athlete. He wasn't the fastest guy, didn't have the best arm, couldn't hit for power, did a lot of things only adequately, had a number of physical limitations, but he did what I believe no one will ever eclipse—collected 4,256 hits—an unbelievable total. Pete Rose did this out of the sheer determination he displayed toward his passion—major league baseball. And hopefully, one day Pete Rose will get the recognition he deserves by being elected to the national Baseball Hall of Fame. Look at Pete Rose, and if you're too young to remember who he is, try to get some tapes and look at how the guy played the game. He showed so much enthusiasm with every at bat, you couldn't believe it. Pete never took a day off. He was an extremely hard-working man. He was relentless in pursuit of his passion—baseball. If you pursue your passion with the same enthusiasm Pete Rose did, you will be successful; I guarantee it.

In Michael Kransy's case he turned his passion for computers into a multibillion-dollar-a-year publicly traded giant: CDW, or Computer Discount Warehouse (www.cdw.com). The company was started by Kransy in 1982 after he placed a three-dollar ad in the *Chicago Tribune* to sell a computer. He sold the computer right away but continued to receive calls about it for days. He realized there was a market for used computers and soon began offering them in large quantities direct to the public.

As is the case with many entrepreneurial ventures, Kransy quickly became overwhelmed by the demand for his computers. But to his credit he managed to keep up, making great service one of the foundations of his success. But the biggest part in his success was his enthusiasm for computers and his love of talking about them with customers. To this day, Kransy's love for computers (his passion) drives CDW in all areas.

For example, Kransy only hires people who love computers and helping customers. Profits are a secondary concern to Kransy. He wants people who are enthusiastic about doing a great job. He knows if people love what they're doing, they'll do a great job and have fun, and the profits will be an automatic byproduct of this.

To promote this "fun" culture, Kransy serves free breakfasts every Tuesday and Thursday. During the summer ice cream is served on hot afternoons. The sprawling headquarters on Milwaukee Avenue in Vernon Hills, Illinois, even offers a 34,000 square foot fitness and child care center that enables employees to work out and play sports while their children are entertained! (I've seen the place personally, and it is awesome.) These types of benefits and the culture Kransy has planted and developed all support his passion for computers and fun. CDW is a great example of what pursuing a passion can do. Imagine yourself doing something you love and making a bunch of money in the process; it can happen and it will *if* you think that way.

George Burns, whose words started off this chapter ("I'd rather be awful at something I love than great at something I hate"), certainly had a passion for acting, and that's probably what enabled him to live ninety-plus years on this earth. He loved his job, and this probably contributed to his long, healthy life.

At Grunder Landscaping Company, we pursue our passions every day. There is nothing that pleases us more than beautifying commercial and residential sites with creative landscaping, and we are addicted to offering great service. We like making people happy with our work. We constantly ask, "Are you happy?" If a client is not happy, we'll make them happy. Why? It is fun! It is our passion. And

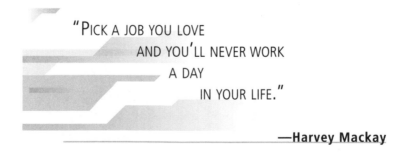

"PICK A JOB YOU LOVE
AND YOU'LL NEVER WORK
A DAY
IN YOUR LIFE."

—**Harvey Mackay**

don't you think our team loves working someplace where the passion is beautifying properties and making clients happy?

The first step to success is unquestionably to pick a passion. There is absolutely no possible way that you will be the best you can be unless you are pursuing or doing something that you love. If you're not doing something you love, it turns into a job—a J-O-B— and, pretty soon, you're coming in at 9:15 and going home at 5:00, and you can't wait for retirement. You'll even contract what I call SIRS—Stuck In a Rut Syndrome. You've become so bored with what you're doing that you can't muster up enough energy to be anything but mediocre at it. Life will be very boring and unfulfilling, and months and years will be wasted.

How Do You Pick a Passion?

Now that I've convinced you to pursue a passion, how do you pick one? Here's a start. I often work with people as a career coach or success coach trying to help them choose something that they think they might excel at (a passion). I tell them to list on a piece of paper all the things they enjoy doing, all the things they enjoy reading about, all of their hobbies, all the things that interest them. After they've listed all of these, and thought it over and added to it for three weeks, I ask them to send that list to me. I then sit down and go through all the things they've listed and try to figure out what potential opportunities there are for them to have a career in the particular areas they have a passion for. Go now and start working on your list!

A tip I share with those working on their passion and other entrepreneurial ideas is to start carrying a Levenger pocket briefcase (available online at www.levenger.com) around with you. This handy little leather notepad holder enables you to carry 3" by 5" cards with you everywhere. Or you can simply carry a pocket-size spiral notebook. Some people I've worked with carry pocket tape recorders. My associate at Grunder Landscaping Company, Paul Stoll, carries a nifty little recording device that he hooks up to his computer, where voice recognition software types up what he said.

The point is, when you come up with an idea, write it down or record it right away. Don't rely on your memory; that is not what successful people do. Ink or pencil on paper is reliable; your memory is not. This way you are always prepared to take advantage of a new thought. If you can catch me without my pocket briefcase, it's worth ten dollars to you. I never go anywhere without it. I've even been known to jot down ideas during church, to my wife's chagrin!

Many business ideas were started on restaurant napkins; this is just a little fancier way of doing it. Starting a business is a long process. You don't want to consider only one idea for your venture. Get a few.

Speaking of ideas—in the back of this book is a critique coupon. You may fax or mail it along with your idea to me for a free critique.

You Know What You Can Do Better Than Anyone Else

I'll never forget a landscaper telling me in the spring of 1987, for example, that there was no money in landscaping and that I should finish up school and get a "real job." Today, when our clean, green trucks pass him, I wonder if he still thinks I should "get a real job." Truth was, I loved landscaping, and despite being told by someone else in business it wouldn't work, I felt it would. I'll also never forget my former accountant telling me in 1988 to get out of the business because I wasn't making money. He said, and I quote,

"Marty, you're robbing Peter to pay Paul, and yes, you are paying for school, but your company has debt." He felt I would be better off shutting down my company and just borrowing money to go to school. Today, I am very grateful for the fire he lit under me, though I wasn't grateful at the time—and immediately switched accountants.

Why did I ignore him? I had a passion for business and landscaping, and I was determined to succeed. I knew I had something, and I was right. He had no idea how determined I was; he underestimated the power of a passion. It was my passion that kicked into high gear and helped me take off. I also knew that just because he was a CPA didn't mean he was smarter than me. Many times we are swayed by someone we put up on a "Godlike" pedestal. Truth is, no one has all the answers. If we all would trust our own conclusions more, you'd realize you're pretty smart yourself. I hope you're feeling confident now and see the power of passion.

If you need any further convincing that even the pros are not always right:

"Everything that can be invented has been invented."
—Director, U.S. Patent Office, 1899

"In 1900, Mercedes-Benz did a study that estimated the worldwide demand for cars would not exceed one million, primarily because of the limitation of available chauffeurs. By 1920 there were eight million Model T's in America."
—Stewart Brand

21

Now, continue to think about what you love to do and begin to consider the potential for that being a business. List **all** the possibilities you can think of first, even the wildest ones, before trying to narrow it down to the most practical ones. Here are several ideas and websites that hopefully will provide examples of inspiration to build your dream. While you are thinking, remember this:

> *"What's worth doing is worth doing for money."*
>
> —Joseph Donohue

Always remember Joseph Donohue's belief that "What's worth doing is worth doing for money."

Your business must be your passion. Just as you can't fake being in love with someone, you can't fake a passion for an idea. And finding your passion is no different than falling in love. You'll know

"IF YOU WANT TO CREATE A BUSINESS,
GO TO A PARTY AND LISTEN.

YOU'LL HEAR PEOPLE COMPLAIN.
EVERY COMPLAINT EQUALS A NEED,
A PROBLEM, A VACUUM.

MEET IT, SOLVE IT, FILL IT—
AND THERE'S YOUR BUSINESS."

—Fred Smith, founder of FedEx

when it happens. Begin to picture yourself daily doing something you love and making money in the process. Wouldn't that be awesome?

What If You Have More Than One Passion?

Let's say you have several passions, but you're not sure which one to pick for your venture, which will work best as a business. Here are a few ideas to help you zero in on this.

First, start reading as many books and magazines you can about successful entrepreneurs. Every single business at one time was one person. They all started out small. True, today entrepreneurs may enter the marketplace quickly and with many employees. But every venture still was the brainchild of one individual. Books like *The Burger King, Built from Scratch,* and *Radical Marketing* are among my favorites. Magazines such as *Inc., Entrepreneur, Network Marketing, Fast Company, Fortune,* and trade journals in the particular field you think you want to be in will teach you a lot. They (and this book) will help you find answers to questions, give you ideas, and inspire you to pursue the entrepreneurial dream. Reading about successful people and how they did it is both educational and inspirational. If you read a book and identify well with the author or the people in the book, try to contact them. Most authors are surprisingly approachable. One such author you might identify well with is Howard Shultz, founder of Starbuck's coffee. He has a great book on tape you can buy and listen to while driving. His audiocassette program is titled *Pour Your Heart into It*. It will show you how powerful passion is in a successful business. Heck, really get into it and go lounge on

SKILL, INTEREST, OR HOBBY	BUSINESS IT COULD BE USED TO START
ANIMALS	
	Pet care
	Pet training
	Grooming
	Pet sitting
	Pet exercising service
	Kennels
	Drive-thru dog & cat fast food
	Pet hotel and country club
	Pet store
	Pet supply catalog (www.petwarehouse.com)
	Pet cemetery
	Home delivery of pet food
	Design, install, and maintain fish tanks
	Horseback riding school
	Horse boarding service
	Horse trainer
	Provide horse-drawn vehicles for tourists, parties, and special events
	Blacksmith
	Writing about animals
	Photographing animals

SKILL, INTEREST, OR HOBBY	BUSINESS IT COULD BE USED TO START
MUSIC	
	Entertainment for corporate parties, weddings, sporting events, etc.
	Marching band for hire
	Serenades for hire
	Provide accompaniment for dance classes
	Start a dancehall
	Music store (www.hauermusic.com)
	Music school
	Buy and sell instruments
	Rent instruments
	Instrument repair store (www.hauermusic.com)
	A school that teaches people how to play an instrument in one month
	Orchestrate, arrange, and write custom music
YOUNG PEOPLE	
	Tutoring services
	Music or sports lessons C
	Learning center
	Day camps
	Provide field trips and day trips
	Amusement park or "play place" for children

SKILL, INTEREST, OR HOBBY	BUSINESS IT COULD BE USED TO START
	Child chauffeuring service
	Chaperone service
	Video/computer game store for young people
	Toy store
	Performer (clown or musician, etc.) for children's parties
	Child photography
	Used children's clothing/equipment swap store
GARDENING	
	Landscaping (www.grunderlandscaping.com)
	Lawn care (www.weedman.com)
	Produce and install sod
	Plan and install water gardens
	Tree trimming
	Tree moving service
	Garden center
	Greenhouse for plants or out-of-season vegetables
	Mail order vegetable stand
	Floral arrangements for special events
	Dried flower decorations

SKILL, INTEREST, OR HOBBY	BUSINESS IT COULD BE USED TO START

Gardening, continued

Interior plantscaping

Identify/diagnose/treat garden pests and
diseases

Vegetable garden planting and maintenance
service

Design and install herb gardens
and window boxes

Teach ways to preserve your crop: canning,
freezing, drying, root cellaring

COMPUTERS

Computer selection specialist

On-site hardware or software training

On-site computer repair/troubleshooting

Computer installation service

Buy and sell used computers

Web design firm
(www.expressions.com)

Network administrator
(www.commsys.com)

Teaching people how to use the Internet

Online research service

SKILL, INTEREST, OR HOBBY	BUSINESS IT COULD BE USED TO START
Computers, continued	Online auctioning service for collectibles, etc.
	Online translation service
COOKING	Restaurant (www.zingermans.com)
	Diner
	Lunch wagon
	Catering
	Made to order cakes/cookie trays
	Bed and breakfast
	Gourmet or special-diet "meals on wheels"
	Write or sell cookbooks
	Food shopping for discriminating customers
	Health and wellness center
	Plan and execute cookouts for groups and gatherings
CRAFT MAKING	Craft and gift making
	A craft store/day care for kids

SKILL, INTEREST, OR HOBBY	BUSINESS IT COULD BE USED TO START

Craft Making, continued

Theme or specialty craft shop

Craft instructor

Renting out kiln time

Craft supply store

Producing craft kits

Organizing and running craft fairs

CARS

Repair shop

Paint shop

Detail shop

Car customizing service

Car cleaning service

Oil changing service

Renovate antique cars

Vehicle reupholstering service

Auto parts store/tire supplier

Search service for hard to find car parts

Machine shop service for vehicles

Towing service

29

SKILL, INTEREST, OR HOBBY	BUSINESS IT COULD BE USED TO START
SEWING	
	Tailoring
	Mending
	Alteration service
	Making draperies
	Custom needlework
	Upholstery
	Sewing pattern design
	Making costumes to order
	Doll clothes specialist
PUBLIC SPEAKING	
	Motivational speaker (www.natebooth.com)
	Speechwriter
	Speechmaking trainer
	Tour guide
	Sports announcer
SELLING/PERSUASION	
	Multi-level marketing groups like Amway, USANA, Nikken.com
	Real estate agent (www.loissutherland.com)

SKILL, INTEREST, OR HOBBY	BUSINESS IT COULD BE USED TO START

Selling/Persuasion, continued

    Manufacturer's representative

    Product demonstrator

    Professional fund-raiser

    Create and run classified ad publication

    Produce commercials or other radio or
        telemarketing (www.studioworks.com)

TRAVEL

    Write travel books or articles

    Conduct guided tours for hobbyists, special interest
        groups

    Trip planning and packing, including
        efficient handling of special problems
        like prescriptions

    Translator, etiquette consultant
        for businesspeople on tour

    Chaperone for traveling children, women,
        handicapped, etc.

    Bonded private special delivery service
        to places that interest you

    Deliver live animals, plants,
        other perishables with special needs

    Independent buyer for specialty shops

SKILL, INTEREST, OR HOBBY	BUSINESS IT COULD BE USED TO START
Travel, continued	
	Product support, repair, installation for international companies
WELDING	
	Manufacturing company
	Custom truck body manufacturing
	Repair shop
	Vehicle frame straightening service
	On-site repair service
	Industrial maintenance service for subscribing companies
	"Rent a welder" service
	Welding demonstrator
TRUCK DRIVING	
	Training school
	Hauling company
	Truck stop parts shop
	Complete "trails to rails to sails" transporting service
	Custom packing and hauling of hard-to-ship products

SKILL, INTEREST, OR HOBBY	BUSINESS IT COULD BE USED TO START

Craft Making, continued

Employment service for truckers with or without their own rigs

Information service for truckers on different states' traffic laws, weight rules, fuel regulations, detours, etc.

FIXING THINGS

Handyman service (www.mrhandyman.com)

Appliance repair

China and glassware repair

Fence repair

Masonry repair

Furniture repair

FINANCE MANAGEMENT

Custom production of no longer produced parts

Running a business, franchise (www.hangars.com)

Starting your own bank

Stockbroker

Financial planner (www.ebs.com)

Finance management service for small businesses

SKILL, INTEREST, OR HOBBY	BUSINESS IT COULD BE USED TO START
FASHION	
	Helping professionals dress
	Find a fashion gap and fill it
	Fashion trend "hotline" newsletter
	Hat shop, including custom hats (www.hatworld.com)
	Ethnic outfit store
	Supply tuxedos and party dresses
	Personal care products supplier
	Makeup supplier and advisor

a couch in a Starbuck's with a café latte and listen to the story on your headphones. Look around while you're in there, and you'll feel the passion Howard had and still has today.

Kaile Warren, Jr. was broke and homeless and had nowhere to go but up. So in 1996 he formed Rent-A-Husband with an old van with the words "Rent-A-Husband" on the side with black electrical tape. He printed fliers and placed them on cars outside buildings where women's divorce support group meetings were held. The gimmick worked, and soon his business was booming. He took his passion for fixing things to the next level.

reality check

Only You Know Best

Remember that "the experts" aren't always right—not even me. Many years ago while I was speaking in Chicago, a young man asked me to look at his business plan. He wanted to start a store that rented out books on tape and sold motivational material like signs and posters. I told him I didn't think there was a market for renting books on tape. Recently while in Chicago, I came across a thriving store that did just what this young man wanted to do. The place was packed! I hope he ignored me, and that is his store. I was too embarrassed to ask the employees who owned it.

Moral of the story? You know your business and your dream better than anyone. Don't let a hotshot consultant, family member, or even another successful entrepreneur shoot it down. Listen to what they have to say, log it away, but keep in mind only you have the ability to see the "forest" through the "trees" in pursuit of your dream or passion. You just might have something that would work. You need to reach a balance between the criticisms and what your heart tells you.

A Fork in My Own Road

In 1986, as a senior at Archbishop Alter High School, in Kettering, Ohio, I had a major decision to make. I did okay in school but certainly didn't set any world records for grade point averages. I graduated 153rd out of 313 students. Now I had to decide what college would I attend and what my major would be. At this time, my business was making around $40,000 per year, which is a lot of money for someone eighteen years old. Should I go to Ohio State University and pursue a degree in land-scape architecture or horticulture and try to learn the technical side of the business? Or should I go to Ohio University and pursue a degree in broadcast journalism, as I was the voice of the Alter Knights basketball team on a radio station that had light bulbs more powerful than it? Or should I go to the University of Dayton, a school near and dear to my heart, my mom's alma mater? I had followed the basketball team there since the late 1970s.

I liked to make money, but I had two passions, two loves. One was landscaping, and the other was sportscasting. I liked the idea of a career in either of these fields very much. But I felt that I had a better opportunity to be a great landscaper than a great sports-caster. There were a lot of people competing for very few sports-casting positions. On the other hand, there were very few landscapers competing for thousands of landscape jobs. I was cer-tain of that. The population of Dayton and its suburbs in 1986 was around 800,000, and I figured at least ten percent of those people, or 80,000, could use landscaping. If I could convince only 80–150, or .1875 percent of those 80,000, to spend $2,000 to $3,000 with me each year, the business would work.

Picking a High-Profit Passion

The idea is to find a passion in which research shows the probability of success is very high.

How might you do this?

1. *Visit with some bankers and ask them what they think of your idea.* Tell them about the business you have in mind. Do they know of any successful companies doing what you

want to do that you could meet with? Do they know of any entrepreneurs whose companies failed that you could interview? Why did those companies fail, or work? Will the bank loan you money? How much money do other companies like yours usually borrow? Do they have any copies of business plans of other companies? Can you read them? Sure, that's a bold question, but if you don't ask, you don't know.

2. *Visit successful companies in this field.* Take trips out of town if necessary to see how other firms in the field you think you want to enter do things. Ask the owner to tell you what to watch for. Ask them if you could see their business plan. Visit small firms and big firms. The small firms will be more realistic to you, but the big firms will serve as your dream. You will be surprised at how open these entrepreneurs will be with you. It is human nature for people to help.

3. *Check bankruptcy records.* Have an inordinate number of firms in the field you have in mind gone out of business? What can your attorney dig up on this? If a lot of businesses go bankrupt in your chosen field, find another field or find out if the reason they failed is something you can fix. My research tells me restaurants, bars, and tech startups have the highest rate of failure.

4. *Ask complete strangers what they think of your idea.* You need to find out if your idea is workable from other people's point of view. I will discuss this kind of research in more detail later. In general a lot of beneficial information can be gathered from it. Ask friends and family if you

wish, but remember they will usually tell you what you want to hear. What you want are people who have an unbiased view and will offer constructive criticism.

5. *Attend seminars and trade shows in your chosen field.* Almost every profession has a trade group that helps promote and improve the industry, and they usually sponsor a trade show and/or seminar. Go to those trade shows and ask those currently in the industry what is good and what is bad about it. Ask them if they think you should go into the industry. And get their card so you can call them later. Ask others in the business or search the web. I am constantly amazed how much information is on the World Wide Web. Network with and meet as many people as possible. You will find very few who don't want to share their successes and failures with you. You may even find a few companies you can hone your skills at.

6. *Look in phone books.* Go to the largest library in your area and look through the yellow pages in the category you're considering. Call some of the companies listed there and act like you're in need of their services. Ask questions, such as, how much does your product or service cost? What are your hours? What is your turnaround time? How long have you been in business? And anything else you'd like to ask. I spent hours in the University of Dayton library gathering information on other companies by reading their yellow pages ads.

The following is a series of questions I would get answers to before selecting a business or investing any money in any business:

1. What is the average revenue per employee in this business? You can find this out from trade associations, which normally have periodic surveys of information like this. You can also check resources like *Robert Morris Annual Statement Studies* (located at your local library). Your banker or accountant may also know the answer to this.

2. What is the average revenue per square foot? This is very important for retail operations, to budget accordingly and compare.

3. What is the average profit margin?

4. What is the average gross margin?

This is a great exercise as you'll see how much money the average company in your venture makes. In fact you may be surprised at how little some entrepreneurs make. In your research you might uncover some other, better ideas for a business. And you very well might avoid a huge mistake. Years ago I thought about opening a retail plant nursery. After a couple of months of research, I realized that financially it was not a viable business for me, because the potential profits were outweighed by the huge risk. I'm sure glad I did that research.

Have More Than One Plan

Even with all of your research, you still should always have more than one plan.

I speak to thousands of people, young and old, every year on the subject of entrepreneurship and success. I enjoy asking the audience what their dreams are. Many young people say they want to be a doctor, a lawyer, or an entrepreneur, but many also say they are going to play professional sports. If you're seventeen years old and 5'9", the likelihood of you playing in the NBA is slim. Go ahead, though, and practice your jump shot, you just might make it. Muggsy Bogues is 5'3" and, was a very good NBA player. However, Muggsy Bogues also has a degree in communication from Wake Forest University (1987) to fall back on. The lesson—always have a back-up plan. Always. That's why cars have spare tires, retirement homes have generators, and even parachutes have back-up parachutes. Whether your entrepreneurial dream requires physical talent such as art, sports, or musicianship or not, make certain you have a Plan B just in case you don't make the NBA. Maybe you could coach in the NBA, be a scout, be a general manager, or even own the team. Most people I coach want to switch from working for a company to working for themselves. They believe they could do something better than their employer is. But the key is to have more than one plan in place. Things don't always work out the way you planned, and if you have a Plan B ready, you can quickly overcome the failure of Plan A.

In the corporate world, they call this scenario planning. This means you put together several plans with triggers in place. If a trigger is released, you go on to the next plan. Here's an example of how an aspiring entrepreneur might go about this:

Plan A: You want to start a home building company. You aim to build two homes next year. But if by March you have no homes under contract, Plan B will kick in.

Plan B: Since you have no new homes under contract, and you need cash flow, you will now offer your talent to existing builders as a subcontractor. This way you will learn more "tricks of the trade," get some cash, and start networking. If you don't get any work like this from builders for whatever reason, Plan C is triggered.

Plan C: Since the first two scenarios didn't work out, you are now on to Plan C. Plan C is to offer home fix-it services (by the way, this is, in my opinion, a great business) and home remodeling. This way, even though you're a little removed from your original dream, you're still in the industry. That's good, you're getting your name out, learning, and you should be having fun.

You probably get the point about planning. I'm a big believer in scenario planning. Always have a back-up plan. You will find as you start researching your entrepreneurial dream that many entrepreneurs are not in the business they originally intended to be. But through a good set of plans, creativity, and persistence, they finally found their passion. Keep in mind you'll miss one hundred percent of the shots you don't take!

Taking a shot or swing at something at least puts your dream in motion. You'll learn so much from this! You should see some of the first landscape jobs we did … boy, were they awful. But it got us started, and I learned a lot. You too can learn a lot and most likely find a viable business by experimenting in areas of your passion. But remember to always have a back-up plan.

Now Do Some Planning

Never be fooled into thinking that only a passion is needed to survive. You've only completed one chapter or step. If business were that easy, we'd all be rich. Much more is needed to be a successful entrepreneur. Many entrepreneurs have lost everything pursuing a passion. Why? No planning, no goals, and quite honestly laziness. Yes, laziness! Success in business is a process. Few are so lucky that their endeavor takes off without months, even years, of planning prior to starting. I knew some unsuspecting entrepreneurs, for instance, who purchased a thriving meat market only to find out once they owned the place that the lease expired in six months. No big deal, they thought, until six months later, they received a notice telling them their lease would not be renewed as a major drugstore bought the property and was tearing the building down and building a new store. The location was so wonderful and affordable that the meat market's success was in large part due to it. They looked for a new location, but the costs to rent the space and outfit the new store prevented them from moving. They went out of business instead and lost a fortune. Better research would have uncovered this problem, but in their rush to become entrepreneurs, they did not ask enough questions.

Take your time and check things out thoroughly. Hire an attorney and an accountant to help you avoid mistakes pursuing your passion. Get a successful entrepreneur on board early as an advisor. They will be able to help you greatly.

Pick a passion to get started and then start your planning. Read on for help with the planning.

chapter three

Set Your Goals

"There are no 'do-overs' in life.
We can only move on from where we are right now;
even if the steps are small; each one moves us
directly into the future."

—Barry J. Farber, TV/radio personality

Now that you're thinking about a passion, or maybe even zeroed in on one, it's time to move on to Step 2—setting your goals.

Getting Started

Many people spend their entire lives talking about what they're going to do. But that's all they do—talk. As the saying goes "talk is cheap." At some point you have to do something, anything to get started on the road to success. Sitting around each day dreaming and talking about it doesn't work. You need to take your passion and make out a plan with some deadlines. A plan outlining your dream with specific, detailed goals is what separates winners from losers.

Later on in this chapter we will discuss a formal business plan, but for now let's just work on getting your dream down on paper.

You're never too young or old to be successful. It doesn't matter where you are in your life; you can start. Forget about the past and start working on the future today. Push the reset button. It is your chance for a do-over. Take one small step or goal at a time starting RIGHT NOW! Since we are just getting started, right now all I want you to do is to draw a picture of what your business will look like. That's right, get out the pencils, crayons, and paper and draw what your dream is. Take fifteen minutes and do it now and come back to this spot once you've completed your picture.

When I was eighteen, I had a highly detailed drawing of what my trucks would look like, and another one of my future office and warehouse. Yet another one of the team that would enable me to realize my dream. And a final one of the house I could afford from my great job. From my own personal experience and my work with others, I know that putting your goals on paper makes them real. True, they are still a dream, but once you put them down, make them visible, you have gotten serious. Having your dreams and

reality check

Putting your goals down on paper makes them real. They are no longer pipe dreams; an action has taken place, and the goal is now a real, live objective. Secondly, writing things down will encourage you to analyze your plan and take action. Studies have shown that fewer than three percent of all people write down their goals. But studies also show if you write down your goals and detail the steps you need to take to achieve them, the chances of achieving your goal are sixty-five to eighty-five percent!

goals in writing and looking at them constantly is one of the most effective methods for achieving them. Why? It forces you to really think about and focus on and work toward achieving those goals.

Once you put your goals in writing, you become more focused on what needs to be done for you to consider yourself successful. Lou Holtz, the legendary football coach, first wrote his goals down in 1966 at age 28. Among the goals he listed were: Become head coach at Notre Dame, win a national championship, meet the president, meet the pope, and skydive. His list of goals had 107 items on it. He has accomplished most of them including meeting the president and the pope and winning a national championship. Holtz says he is so focused on accomplishing goals he doesn't like to sleep. Now there's a goal-oriented man!

You need to think deeply about your goals, think them through thoroughly. You are going to be in pursuit of them for many years, most likely.

Don't Put Money First

The goals should be consistent with your personal values too. Many people get greedy and bend the rules to be successful. Don't do this. Be honest always. ALWAYS! There is no such thing as "mostly honest." You're either honest, or you're not. Here is probably the best piece of advice you will get in this entire book—treat others the way you want to be treated, always telling the truth. Never deviate from this, and you will be rewarded. If you treat people the way you want to be treated and are honest, clients will buy from you, employees will want to work for you, and your friends and family will want to be around you and will help you.

reality check

Nine to five doesn't work for aspiring entrepreneurs. Your entrepreneurial dream will often include late nights and missed family functions because your business controls you so. There will also be failures. (Yes, failures. Not everything will be perfect, and many times you'll learn more from the things that go wrong than the things that go right.) So make certain that all the significant people in your life know what your goal is. If you're married, your spouse must know and support your goal and the sacrifices that must be made to achieve it. If you have children, they must know and understand you will try not to miss their school plays, games, or other significant events, but you're not going to be home early every night. The business is not more important than the family, but entrepreneurs, especially new ones, can't go home at five, and they don't get weekends off.

I have come across people whose only goal was to make money. They pursued this goal without consideration for anything else. Money alone is not good enough. You need a deeper reason than that. Don't get me wrong; every day I wake up and go to work with a goal of making money, but it is about number four on my list. Number one is to help people; number two is to be honest and protect my reputation in the process; number three is to have fun; and number four is to make money.

The neat thing about my goals being as such is I don't have to think about making money—it happens naturally. One of my mentors, Clay Mathile, sold his company (Iams) for over 2 billion dollars to Procter & Gamble in 1999! Not once did I ever hear Clay place the quest for money at the top of the list. From my observation he put the well-being of cats and dogs first, his employees a close second, and money came third. Now, Clay is a brilliant businessman who has helped hundreds of entrepreneurs achieve financial prosperity. However, in all my meetings and conversations with him, all the classes his entrepreneurial school puts on, and in everything I can see and observe, he does not say nor teach you to make money your number one focus. Money is the output of a well-oiled machine. The better the machine works, the more money you'll make. So focus on the machine. Clay often speaks of focus. He advised me to focus on building the best landscaping company in the U.S. and to stay committed to that. He went on to tell me that many businesses fail because of a lack of focus. We'll get into this deeply in Chapter 7. But for now you need to really zero in on your goals and get a plan to achieve them.

I have worked with countless aspiring entrepreneurs who can show me highly detailed drawings of their proposed store, warehouse, product, or office. They can show me elaborate business plans with forecasts of sales and earnings. They can even show me organizational charts and creative marketing plans detailing who they'll sell their product or service to and how. This is great, but something more basic is needed as well. I always force them to search for deeper and more basic goals.

Why Do You Want to Be an Entrepreneur?

First, you need to be able to say why *you* personally are starting your own business. Do you want more free time? If the answer is yes, choose something other than entrepreneurship. Eventually, if you

47

reality check

The recent success of dot com companies has many believing they'll make millions overnight. For every dot com that makes it, several fail. In general, as your mom or dad probably told you when you were a teenager, "If it sounds too good to be true, it is." Those who get rich quick are a very select, risk-taking few. Don't go into a new business thinking you'll get rich quick. Most successful entrepreneurs made money after years of struggles and commitment to a goal. They took small, steady steps to wealth. The race to success is a marathon, not a sprint.

fully learn how to run a business and how to delegate, you may be able to have more free time (a stage I'm starting to get to after eighteen years!). But that will take years of practice and installing foolproof systems. Being an entrepreneur is a very time-consuming venture.

Do you want to get rich? You can get rich but not quickly; it will take time. An entrepreneur in Missouri I have worked with since his initial startup in 1997 told me he wanted to make one thousand dollars a week by December of 1999. We set up his business together so he could do this. It was a very realistic and attainable goal. Today he makes two times that!

The reason I am asking you to look deeper is that a lot of aspiring entrepreneurs get ankle deep in problems before they find out they really don't like being an entrepreneur. They end up in this position because they skip analyzing their personal goals—the basics, the simple things no one thinks of. I've seen restaurants and retail operations go out of business because their owners were too caught up in the romance of running their own business to realize why they really wanted to run their own business.

Do you want to have fun? Who doesn't, right? Sure, you want to have fun. I started Grunder Landscaping Company in 1983 as Grunder Lawn Service to make $40,000 to pay for a college education and to have fun. I then went out and tried to find help so I could do just that. I have since built on those very basic goals and today have a successful landscaping company. My simple goals were an excellent start. I only wish I could tell you I knew what I was doing then; I didn't. I was just very lucky and so are you to now know this. Come up with a simple, attainable goal and post that goal everywhere.

Ask yourself, "What do I want out of this business?" Once you've answered that, ask several people in your family, your friends, other entrepreneurs, your attorney, and your accountant their opinion of the answer. Remember though, many family and friends don't know anything about business. And just because Uncle Bill has a business doesn't mean he is an expert. All of these people, however, can point out problems your business may make for your family and personal life.

Once you've determined your personal goals, and made sure they're reasonable and don't create any conflicts for you, your next goal should center on building a world-class service or product. The product or service should be designed to bring satisfaction to your clients if not sheer delight. Do this and set secondary goals up toward this, and you'll see the money come rolling in.

Make Short-Term and Long-Term Goals

I like to see my clients put together a plan that has both short-term and long-term goals. Your short-term goals should be ones you want to attain within a year, and your long-term goals the ones it will take longer to achieve. All of these goals should contribute toward your ultimate goal. The ultimate goal would be defined as the objective that when achieved will make you feel like you've arrived at the top. On the short-term list should be things you want and need to accomplish in the next year that are critical to your business being a success initially. On the long-term list should be objectives to be accomplished in the next two to ten years that are milestones toward that ultimate goal.

Make Your Goals Measurable

Whenever possible, make your goals measurable. That's why they keep score in a sports game, folks. And make your goals realistic. If you were just getting started in selling real estate, it would be unrealistic to put "Sell three million dollars' worth of real estate in your first year." But a million dollars' worth, well, that might be attainable, so make sure your goal is attainable. Even if it is a little stretch, put it down. That's okay. Nothing will be more frustrating than to pick a goal that is absolutely impossible.

Five Kinds of Goals to Make

You have a general idea of where you want to go. The mystery lies in how you're going to get there. There are five kinds of goals you should form now to make things clearer. First is financial goals.

Financial Goals

How much money do you want to make? How much do you **have** to make? (There is a difference.) How much money will you need to start your venture? Where will you get it? Let's look at each of these now in some detail.

reality check

It is critical that your personal beliefs don't clash with your business goals. This includes your religious beliefs, your political beliefs, and your ethics, to name a few. In my town, for instance, a beautiful new car wash opened up. It has a café inside it and all the latest equipment. The location is superb, and it looks as if it would be an excellent little business. But there is one big problem—they are closed Saturdays because the owners' religion prohibits them from working then. Although this is an admirable stance they've taken, ask yourself when do you get your car washed? Most common answer? Probably Saturday or Sunday. How does this car wash expect to be profitable being closed on Saturdays? Only time will tell, but I don't think it will work. Why? The main reason is the conflict of the goal of the business to be profitable and the goal of the owners to not work Saturdays. People flock to car washes on Saturdays. Make sure your personal goals don't conflict with your business goals; if they do, find another business.

reality check

Many times, I work with small business owners who have sales in their company of around $300,000 to $500,000 a year. I ask them what their goal is, and they say, "Next year I want to do $1,000,000." Well, that might be possible, but if you have twelve employees, and you're doing $500,000 now, is it realistic to think that you can get these same employees to produce $1,000,000 the following year? It's not likely and still keep your service and your quality at the levels that you will need to grow your business. What about twenty-four people doing $1,000,000? That may be possible but can you keep your quality up? Remember, an unhappy client will tell seven people. A happy client will tell two. Doing poor work is the worst possible thing you can do for your business. Uncontrolled growth is one of the most common reasons for the demise of businesses. Just because sales grow does not automatically make profits grow.

How much money do you want and have to make?

Let's start there. If you or your family needs $40,000 in net dollars to make the mortgage payment, the car payments, and meet all other expenses, then see if your venture can provide that. Sure, you probably want to make four times that. But very few new businesses can provide that much right off the bat. The many kinds of planning I discuss in this chapter can help you see how realistic your needs and your dreams are here.

How much money will you need?

This is where you'll need some help. I would strongly suggest you seek out the wealth of free resources available in your town, such as: (1) SCORE; (2) the chamber of commerce; and (3) uni-

reality check

Many people are way too optimistic about what they intend to make. Get real! If you are making $38,000 a year as a plumber for a successful operation, it's not realistic to think you're going to make $120,000 your first year in business. The word "make" means what will your profit after expenses be, not what will you gross. There is an expression used by successful entrepreneurs that says, "Don't show me your top line (gross sales), show me your bottom line (profit)." If you made $38,000 last year, let's shoot for $38,000 in year one. That may not be what you want to make, but you probably can't afford to make much less than that. If you are going to start your own business because you need more money right away, don't! This is way too much pressure to put on yourself. Also, if you were pulling in $100,000 as vice president of a plumbing company, don't think you'll make that the first year either. Entrepreneurship often involves many expenses that you may have never even thought of. In other words, it costs a lot of money to be self-employed. For example, all those business lunches you used to turn in on your expense report? Well, those now come out of your wallet! You will need to cut back on some things for a while. Very few businesses can open their doors and reach optimum capacity, efficiency, and profitability right away.

versities. SCORE is the Service Corps of Retired Executives (www.score.org). These retired executives are bright, experienced mentors you can ask for free help. Look in the business white pages, call your local chapter, and ask what they offer. Most cities have a chamber of commerce whose sole mission is to improve business in their region. Go in and see their small business development expert. The free advice and services they have to offer should be taken advantage of.

Universities are, in my opinion, the best source of information of all. Unfortunately, most aspiring entrepreneurs don't know what they have to offer, are too lazy to use it, or are afraid to ask for help. Go to the nearest college or university and talk to the dean or associate dean of the business school and tell them about your proposed venture. Ask them if there is anything about it their school could help you with. Many universities will allow their students to perform market research, strategic management planning, and financial planning (more on this shortly) as part of their class work.

Financial planning is your overall budget for your venture. As we just discussed, how much money will you need, and what are your revenue projections? This is all part of the business plan a university or college business school can help put together. This usually is not only inexpensive but extremely helpful and well done. The students work hard doing all kinds of usually high-quality work that you could not afford otherwise. If you don't want to pursue this route, talk to your accountant.

Strategic management planning may sound a little intimidating, but it is really just the answers to three questions: Who are you now? Who do you want to be? And, finally—this is the tough part— how are you going to get where you want to be?

Finding a banker—or more than one

I am an advocate of smaller banks for small startups. Smaller hometown banks tend to be run by people who listen better. Problem is, these small banks are becoming hard to find with all the consolidation going on. Most small banks themselves are rather entrepreneurial by nature. Call a small bank and say something like this, "Hi! I'm Ellen Entrepreneur, an aspiring entrepreneur. Can I talk to you for a half hour sometime soon about my venture?" It is better to set up an appointment so you and the banker have a chance to get to know each other. Go into the bank and share your plan with the banker. Let this banker see your enthusiasm for your endeavor. Show him or her your ideas and all the thought you've put into this venture. Once this relationship has been established, go through the process again, only this time with a big bank. Why? Because big banks have many great resources too!

Other sources of startup capital

Banks are not the only place you can go for financing. Here's a list and description of some other sources that might help you get your venture off the ground.

Small Business Administration (SBA) Go to their website at www.sba.gov. This federal agency was founded in 1953 under the Eisenhower presidency to help people like you and me finance new and existing businesses. The SBA does not loan the money directly. They back or guarantee the loan from the bank. Since the government is involved, the bank has little risk and consequently offers lower interest rates.

Since 1953 nearly 20 million small businesses have received direct or indirect assistance from the SBA. It is considered to be the government's most cost-effective economic development tool. In

reality check

Remember again, that if you do the other kinds of planning I describe in this chapter, your financial goals should fall in place automatically. It makes little sense to make your financial goals the driving force because this tells you nothing about how those goals are going to be met.

Let me clarify. If you make your financial goals your main focus, if all decisions are based on financial considerations, you will run into trouble and may never achieve your dream. For example, a new country club in my town is obviously focused primarily on their financial goals. How do I know? Everything they do is focused on attracting business and cutting costs. They practically beg for you to join. But in their haste to make their numbers they are understaffed. They nickel and dime you for everything and even argue with you when you inquire about getting a credit for a bad meal or bad service. They have yet to survey their members and ask if they are happy. I tell my friends not to join because they have a lot of improvements to make. It is a shame because the facility is first class and the concept excellent, but their implementation and effort to make money tarnish the club and prohibit word-of-mouth advertising.

I am **not** saying financial goals aren't important. What I am saying is make certain client satisfaction is the main priority and be fiscally responsible in the process.

fact, the SBA is the largest single financial backer in the U.S., with over 45 billion dollars in loans backed to aid businesses across the nation. There are several types of finance options available from them. They even have programs designed to help women and minorities start or grow businesses. Your local chamber of commerce may be able to help direct you through the SBA's process. Companies such as Ben & Jerry's Ice Cream and Nike are two SBA success stories. Amazingly, many people don't even know what the SBA is. I do. In 1995 and 1997 I was named Young Entrepreneur of the Year in the State of Ohio by them!

When credit markets tighten due to economic slowdowns, SBA loans become very popular. Repayment terms can be as long as twenty-five years. The drawback of SBA loans is they take a lot of time and documentation to secure. There are bankers who specialize in SBA loans and know how to help you. Get a referral from your local SBA district office or find a list of preferred lenders at www.sba.gov. However, not even a note from the President of the U.S. will speed up this process. I for one don't think that all this planning is a bad thing. The more time you spend thinking about what you're trying to do, the fewer mistakes you'll make.

Look in your area for an SBA seminar and go to it. You might be surprised what you can get from the SBA. Or call them at 1-800-UASKSBA. (Don't feel bad about calling; you pay for this service with your taxes.)

Small Business Investment Corporation (SBIC), Community Capital Development Corporation, port authorities, and other public agencies Again, your local chamber of commerce should be able to provide you with a list of other agencies that help

reality check

You cannot have too many banking relationships. Keep in mind that you will need money to fund your venture. The more sources you have, the more secure you'll be. You never know when the banker who worked with you for five years may change professions, and there goes all that trust and rapport. You also never know when you may develop a problem with your banker. It is smart business to not be reliant on one banker—try to line up at least two.

It will keep your bankers on their toes if you ask for an interest rate quote on money for a new van for instance, by saying, "Can you give me a rate quote for a new van? I'm seeing who's got the best deal."

Also, if you think you need a $25,000 line of credit, ask for $35,000. It is always better to have more money available than you think you need now. You just have to be disciplined enough not to spend all this money.

Through the years I have always kept in contact with my bankers, meeting with them regularly. It's hard for your banker to help you if the only time you call him or her is when you're in trouble. Ask yourself what your opinion is of friends who only call you when they're in trouble. Your banker will learn to trust and admire you for keeping them informed. Contrary to common stereotypes here, I've found bankers to be very helpful. A good relationship with bankers has been a big key to my success, especially early on when I really needed money.

finance small business startups. Many of the above-mentioned are also backed by the SBA but have somewhat more flexible requirements. Or go to the World Wide Web and enter financing in the search engine. Here are two sites to check out: www.ccdcorp.org and www.washingtoncash.org.

"Angel" investors   This is one of my favorite types of financing. Just as angels seem to come from nowhere and answer your prayers, sometimes angel investors help people who can't get help from other places. The few angel groups I have seen in action were made up of ordinary, everyday entrepreneurs. There are groups like these in Dayton, Ohio made up of retired entrepreneurs who love to help other entrepreneurs. Why? Number one, helping is fun. And secondly, most successful entrepreneurs were without funding at one time, too! So they tend to be understanding. You won't be able to secure financing from them, either, without a plan, but they will listen. Again, ask your local chamber of commerce for help finding these people. They normally keep a low profile and network with others to get the word out.

Venture capital   Venture capital comes from funds and groups that invest in new startups or companies trying to grow. A business plan is needed here, too, and normally these groups are tough to sell to. Why? They are typically made up of smart, wealthy businesspeople who became successful by making and executing a plan. If you can't, in one minute, explain to them your business and its profit potential, you will probably not get them to invest. They are generally no-nonsense; however, they will take huge chances if your plan is well done, and a big payday is possible. Some of the wealthiest people in the world got there by being venture capitalists.

Credit cards   Credit cards are a very expensive way to finance a business. I don't recommend them, but they are an option. In general they are an emergency form of financing. Early on in my venture, there were times when credit cards enabled me to pay my employees, make a truck payment, buy plants, and even buy dinner. Get a credit card, but use it only as a last resort. Remember, it all has to be paid back sometime, with interest, of course! So, if you get one, at least carry one with a low interest rate, and always be looking for lower rates.

Friends and relatives This is often the easiest way to get financing, but also the worst, in my opinion. If you borrow from friends and family, you put yourself in a bad position. When you take someone's money, you give them license to be involved in your business whether you like it or not. What if the business doesn't do well? What if your family or friends lose their investment? Or even if the business does well—do you want to be continually scrutinized and questioned at Thanksgiving dinner? All in all I would strongly recommend you rely on financing from sources other than friends and family. If your venture is well thought out, many of the previously mentioned financing avenues should be available and relatives not needed.

To improve your chances of financing

Okay, now you know where to "go for dough." Here are some things that will improve your chances of getting it:

1. An income statement and balance sheet prepared by your accountant. It needs to be current, and I suggest employing a CPA or Certified Public Accountant rather than a public accountant. The CPA designation is not easy to attain, and all CPAs are required to participate in continuing education

yearly to keep that designation. It is a sign of expertise, and in this area it is needed! It is also a very good idea to retain this CPA and take him or her with you to convince lenders to give you the money.

2. A schedule that lists and describes any debt you may have.

3. A schedule showing your current receivables and payables and when they are or were due. This is commonly referred to as an "aging schedule."

4. A complete detailed business plan.

5. A brief but concise summary of your future and current plans for the business including **realistic** projections of revenues

reality check

Don't expect to get money from any lenders without taking some personal risks. I had a client of mine tell me how disappointed he was to not get financing from the bank. He said the bank wanted him to put his house equity up for collateral. He told them, "No way, I could be out on the street if this fails!" My response to him was, "Welcome to the entrepreneurial world." I told him, and I'll tell you—If you aren't willing to put your own personal resources on the line, how can you expect anyone else to? An unwillingness to risk your own money certainly doesn't show confidence on your part that the venture will work, so why should and costs. Many investors want to quickly get to the point. If they like the summary and act intrigued, they'll read the plan.

6.   The past five years' personal and business tax returns.

The basic message here is to get yourself a business plan in writing that details all of the above. Ask around for a person who helps aspiring entrepreneurs put together business plans. There are also books on the subject available at bookstores and libraries.

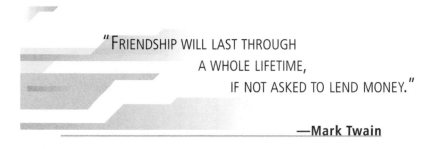

"FRIENDSHIP WILL LAST THROUGH
A WHOLE LIFETIME,
IF NOT ASKED TO LEND MONEY."

—**Mark Twain**

Marketing Goals

Now you need some marketing goals. Who will or can use your product or service? Why will they? This is an excellent question because the answer to this question may uncover an excellent marketing campaign. How will buyers find you; how will you let them know? This area is another that a local college or university can help you with. What are you going to call your company? Where will it be located? If your venture is a retail one, location is very important. These goals are ones you must work extremely hard on. All the money in the world and even a great product don't guarantee success. You must have buyers for your product and/or service. The questions "Who will buy this?" and "Why will they buy it?" need to be asked over and over again.

Otherwise you may end up with a product that no one wants, which is a problem with a lot of businesses. Some people call this "the field of dreams philosophy." The saying comes from the movie *Field of Dreams*, starring Kevin Costner. Costner plays Ray Kinsella, a simple farmer in Iowa, who blows his life savings to build a real baseball diamond in a cornfield at his farm. His dream is inspired and guided by a mysterious voice that tells Costner, "If you build it, they will come." That works great in Hollywood, but neither business nor life is like that. You have to research if there is a market for your product or service. That is a lesson many entrepreneurs learn the hard way. Many restaurants fail because of this. Just ask your banker. Just because you build something doesn't mean that others will come and support it financially. I've seen many great ideas fail because people just weren't interested in the product, or the location of the retail operation was poor.

Let me give you a few examples. I worked with a nice man once who spent over $200,000 on a sophisticated truck that could install mulch on landscapes quickly and efficiently. It is really a

reality check

All of the forms of financing we've discussed will come down to these questions: (1) What's the money being used for? (2) What is the borrower putting at risk? (3) How will the borrower pay it back? If you have the right answers for these questions, you will get the money.

neat piece of equipment that replaces several men with wheel-barrows. The idea is that instead of six people with wheelbarrows spreading mulch, you hire this man with his truck and mulch blower to do it faster and cheaper. Sounds like a winner, right? Problem was, this man skipped the market research part and called me to help him generate business to help pay for the monstrous machine. Had he gone through the market research step, he would have either identified several markets for his mulch machine or realized it was a tough thing to sell. Now with a $230,000 machine already purchased, he found there might not be enough work for it. Not a good feeling and it was probably avoidable. It was "probably" avoidable because even if market research says "go" on something, this doesn't guarantee it will work either. It just increases your chances for success and reduces stress.

Here's another example. If you were planning on opening a consignment store for children's clothes, it would be critical to know how many children lived within ten miles of the store. If the town you're in has mostly retirees, your venture will not work. This may seem obvious to you, but I have seen many aspiring entrepreneurs so blinded by the dream of running their own businesses they forget the obvious. Do your homework.

There are several ways to gather market intelligence. One is focus groups. Focus groups are a collection of people (potential customers) you get together to ask questions. Focus groups can be excellent, but they are not always accurate as people can be swayed by what others in the group say. Another way to do market research is by in-person or phone interviews. This is when you or someone you hire asks questions of consumers, such as what brand of beer do you drink? Or who currently cleans your carpets? You have probably seen or been a part of one of these interviews. These surveys can be fairly inexpensive if you do the work yourself. A mail questionnaire is a form with specific questions on it. These are also fairly inexpensive to do, but many people will throw them out, and your response rate is typically low. Research like the above will reveal some or all of the following:

- What are other companies (competitors) charging for the product or service you would like to offer?

- What is the total volume of business available in your marketplace?

- Who are your competitors?

- What are the current needs in your marketplace?

Doing a thorough job of researching your industry and competition is a very important step to take. Here are several online resources that will make the process a little more manageable. I have used most of them and suggest you spend some time looking at them.

Sites that provide free information on companies and industries, statistics and demographics, as well as tons of great information.

Hoover's Online
www.hoovers.com

Timely and detailed information on more than 50,000 public and private companies

Galileo Internet Resources
www.usg.edu/galileo

A listing of company directories and other competitive analysis sites on the Internet

Michigan State University's MSU-CIBER
globaledge.msu.edu

U.S. and international news and periodicals, statistical data and information resources, international trade information, company directories, and much more

Department of Labor
www.dol.gov

Provides information on labor law.

Environmental Protection Agency (EPA)
www.epa.gov/smallbusiness

Don't ignore environmental regulations in your planning.

U.S. Business Advisor
www.business.gov

Tons of information on starting a business, marketing it, tax laws, and regulations.

Corporate Information
www.corporate information.com

Provides U.S. and international company information, including research reports, company profiles, earnings information, and analyst reports

Company Sleuth
www.companysleuth.com

Monitors up to fifty companies for you

Public Record Databases
www.pac-info.com

Private company resources, compiled by Pacific Information Resources, Inc.

Investigative Resources International
www.factfind.com

Links to searchable databases and research sites, including newspapers, journals, NGOs, privacy & security information, open source records, public agencies, legal information, and more

U.S. Post Office
www.usps.com/smallbiz

There is a lot of helpful information here that may be insightful to you when looking for ways to market your business.

U.S. Census Bureau
www.census.gov

A wealth of information on everything from state demographics to average sales of businesses in your community to stats compiled in the 1997 Economic Census

Federal Statistics
www.fedstats.gov

The gateway to statistics from over one hundred U.S. federal agencies

Annual Reports Library
www.annualreportslibrary.com

Search more than 500,000 annual reports, going back thirty years in financial history. Even if you are small, there is a lot to learn here. After all, at one time just about every company was a small start-up too!

Barron's Annual Report Service
barronsonline.ar.wilink.com

A service that gives you access to annual reports, for select companies, by World Investor Link and Barron's Online.

State Data Center Program
www.census.gov

A cooperative program between the states and the Census Bureau. The Business and Industry Data Center Program also found here is intended to meet the needs of local business communities for economic data.

International Data Base
www.census.gov/ipc/www/idbnew.html

Statistical tables of demographic and socioeconomic data for 227 countries and areas of the world

Internet Public Library Regional & Country Information Resources
www.ipl.org

Resources related to a specific nation or region, including topics such as geography, modern-day history and current events, directories, maps, national libraries, and general reference sites

List of Industry Associations
www.inc.com

Inc.com's compilation of links to industry associations. A great place to learn!

Entreworld
www.entreworld.org

A product of the Ewing Marion Kauffman Foundation. This website's sole purpose is to help aspiring entrepreneurs.

Research services that will charge a fee

Forrester Research
www.forrester.com

Market research and reports

Jupiter Research
www.jupiterresearch.com

Market research and reports

Gartner
www.gartner.com

Market research and reports

Electric Library
www.elibrary.com

For a small fee, will search the contents of newspapers, magazines, television and radio transcripts for stories of interest to your company

Dun & Bradstreet
www.dnb.com

Credit reports including information on specific companies—amount of sales, number of employees, type of customers, ownership, loans, liens, and judgments. You can order reports online for a fee, or sign up to use the service regularly.

Lexis-Nexis
www.lexisnexis.com

One of the best-known resources for information searches of all kinds—includes searchable access to over three billion documents from thousands of sources. And their corporate headquarters is right across the highway from me!

Management Goals

Now for some management goals. Who will help you when you need help? What will you do yourself, and what will you outsource? Who will be your accountant? Your attorney? Who will be your mentors? (See Chapter 5.) What will the "process" of your business be? In

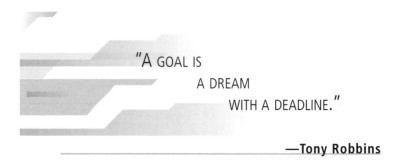

"A GOAL IS
A DREAM
WITH A DEADLINE."

—Tony Robbins

other words, do you have a flow chart that shows exactly how you will go about doing what you do? Do you have an organizational chart? When are you going to start? What does your business plan look like? Who will implement your strategic plan? How are you going to get out if you need to? There is a chance your venture won't work or that you may want to sell it. As you progress, keep this in mind.

Strategic management planning

This is a very important part of your management goals. As I said before, strategic management planning reduced to its simplest form is determining who you are, where you want to go, and how are you going to get there. Strategic management planning has enabled countless companies to succeed.

There is no way I can describe the whole process here. There are entire books devoted to this process. But I can tell you a strategic plan is similar to the road map you use when you go on vacation.

With strategic planning, I have a very good idea of where I'm going every day. I have planned my next few years out, and my team knows what our focus is and where we are headed. A well-organized team works efficiently toward a common goal. A disorganized company loses money by wasting effort and in the process frustrates your team.

Remember again, that failing to plan is planning to fail. Make sure you spend some time planning. To learn more about strategic planning, read *Team Based Strategic Planning* by C. Davis Fogg.

Once you have your plan, follow it closely.

Time Goals

Identifying your goals clearly is one big step toward achieving them. Most goals will also be easier to meet if you give them a time line: some kind of deadline or time frame for accomplishment. This doesn't have to be so precise that it's stress-producing, but it will help a lot, for example, to decide that A, B, and C will need to be done in the next ninety days, L, M, and N, in the next six months, and X, Y, and Z before the year is out. If a particular goal is tied to a very specific date, then make that known.

71

I do this by writing down all my goals on 3" x 5" cards that I carry with me at all times. Every evening before I go to bed, I review my goal cards and my calendar, which I keep on a Palm Pilot personal organizer. A goal that I have placed a deadline on gets entered as an appointment on my calendar. These two steps help keep me focused on what I need to do to be successful. You need to do this.

For years I spun my wheels, seemingly never getting where I wanted to or could. Then I started writing my goals down on paper and attaching deadlines to them, and to my surprise I started to grow my business and make money. I do this faithfully today as I continue to whittle away at my goals.

Your Personal Goals

As noted earlier, it is critical that your personal goals not conflict with business goals. And family needs to be considered. After all, what's the point of working hard and creating a business if you have no one to share it with? Ask yourself this question "Would you rather be rich, successful, and lonely—or rich, successful, and sur-

reality check

Hall of Fame football player Michael Singletary has his family's mission statement posted in the foyer of his home for all to see. Businesses do it, why can't families? The truth is if we treated our clients the way we treat our families and often ourselves, we'd all be bankrupt. At some point you must slow down and do something for yourself and your family.

rounded by a family?" I think that's an easy question to answer. Would you like to be rich and healthy or rich and sickly?

So with that said, please work on your personal goals as well. Put in writing where you want to be in six months, one year, two years, three years, five years, and ten years in your non-business life. For example, this could be an aspiring entrepreneur's personal goal list:

DEADLINE	GOAL
Six months	Be able to run two miles twice a week Take Mom and Dad to dinner every other month Go to doctor and get a physical
One year	Lose fifteen pounds Be able to run five miles Go on vacation with Mom and Dad
Two years	Meet my future spouse Learn how to ballroom dance
Three years	Be married Buy a house
Five years	Have children Volunteer at church
Ten years	Be debt free

Announce Your Goals Now!

We all need help achieving our goals. Hence, many professional speakers, including myself, have become quite successful teaching people how to achieve a goal. But every speaker has his own ideas. Case in point, I was speaking in Portland, Oregon, once and followed an attractive, middle-aged woman who was a highly regarded speaker on goal setting and success. Most times I have no idea what other speakers at conferences I present at are going to say in their talks. And, once in a while, I follow speakers whose message is completely contradicted by mine. None will ever be more contradictory than the story I'm about to share with you.

At 9:55 a.m. on this warm October day she advised the audience to keep your goals to yourself and maybe two VIPs in your life. Her reasoning was that if you tell everyone your goal, you're only going to cause yourself great anxiety and emotional letdown as most people can't achieve their goals. And then these poor people become so embarrassed at their failure, they're never the same as they must repeatedly explain what didn't work out. I couldn't believe what I was hearing, but she said it so emphatically, I'm certain she meant it. She concluded her talk and received warm applause; they really liked her. I thought she was an excellent

reality check

Your plan can and will change as you pursue your goals, but don't let procrastination make you change your plan. Only new ideas or additions should change your plan.

speaker, but her concluding message was terrible; in fact, I couldn't wait to get to the podium to prove her wrong.

At 10:05 I jumped on stage and said, "It's great to be here, and I'm here to completely contradict what you heard at 9:55. You see, the organizers of this event want you to be exposed to all kinds of ideas." I then went through my whole talk on goal setting and achieving. The audience was really into it, but now for the close. I begged the audience to tell everyone and anyone who'd listen what their goals were. "You need to announce your goals everywhere you go for a couple of reasons," I said. "First of all, to get help. By telling people what you want to do, you will get help. For example, if you tell the man you met at the movie theater you want to start your own home remodeling business, he might refer you a client or become a client. Second, how do you expect your family, friends, coworkers, or others to help you if they don't know what you're trying to do? Tell anyone who will listen what your goals are. I firmly believe that telling others what your goals are will help you. Each time you tell others about your goal, you are reminded that you need to do it. Winners get things they say they're going to do done! Losers are afraid to announce what they're going to do because self-doubt has crept into their life. So tell everyone who will listen what your goals are; it will motivate you to get them accomplished."

I closed my talk and received a standing ovation. This told me the audience liked my approach to achieving goals even better than that of the nice woman who spoke before me. Trust me, tell anyone who will listen what your goals are—you are sure to get them accomplished if you do. If you don't have the courage to talk about your goals with strangers, I don't think you're ready to pursue those goals just yet. You probably need more proof you can do what you want to do.

reality check

Steps like those I've just outlined need to be taken. I've seen many ventures go bankrupt from something that could have been avoided. You must be patient with the planning of your business. You will enjoy these visits and this research. Resist the urge to take the plunge before you've done your homework. Remember, success is a process, a marathon, not a sprint! The more time you take planning, the better your chances are to succeed. According to a *Smart Money* magazine study, more than one half of all new businesses fold within one year.

The Small Business Administration tracked companies over a ten-year period to see how many were still in business. These businesses, all created in 1976, were of varying sizes, from one employee up. Check out these figures.

Percentage of businesses still in operation among:

	Companies of all sizes, soloists included	Companies that hired one to four people	Companies that hired five or more people
After 2 years	76%	92%	94%
After 4 years	47%	80%	87%
After 6 years	38%	76%	79%
After 8 years	29%	53%	70%
After 10 years	21%	41%	62%

Source: U.S. Small Business Administration, *The State of Small Business: A Report of the President*, 1997. Year ten percentages are estimated by the SBA.

What does this show? Most businesses fail! Companies that plan will improve their chances of success. When half of all businesses close after four years, you better do the one thing that can improve your chances—PLAN! Take your time, be patient, and be careful. This advice alone can help you be successful.

Does a Goal Seem Hard to Reach?

Look at the goals that seem impossible to conquer, but you would like to accomplish. Things you may to this point in your life have only dreamed of. Sit down with your mastermind group (see Chapter 5—Surround Yourself with Winners), your group of winners, and brainstorm ways that you can do it.

Many times reflecting back on how far you've come in the past five to ten years can be a very beneficial exercise. When I'm feeling like I haven't accomplished as much as I should, I think back. In 2001 many of our gross sales totals for a month were more than Grunder Landscaping did in all of 1991! In 1994 we had eleven team members; today we have forty-five. In 1996 I did two out-of-town speaking engagements; today I do twenty times that!

Where were you four years ago? What have you learned? What are you better at now? I am confident you will find you've accomplished much and will realize quietly you have been successful.

Reward Yourself for Accomplishment!

Be sure to celebrate any and all accomplishments on the way to reaching your goal. Several times a year, we have boot camps at the Winner's Circle where we bring in small business owners from all over the country to a resort or conference center and hold an intensive three-day seminar. At these boot camps we give our attendees a whole new arsenal of marketing and management ideas, and motivation to take back to their part of the world. Every time I have one of these, my staff wonders how we'll get fifty or a hundred people to Dayton or wherever we're having it, but I always do it. How do I

GOAL	OBJECTIVE	REWARD
1. Visit with banker and ask:		
	1. If idea is financeable	
	2. Ask what percentage of plumbers make it	
	3. Ask what to watch for	
	4. What do plumbers need for capital?	
		Hot fudge sundae
2. Visit with Korrect Plumbing in Dayton, Ohio		
	1. Tour facilities	
	2. Ask for advice	
	Dinner with wife at favorite restaurant	
Visit with J. Jones Plumbing in Phoenix, Arizona		
		See Phoenix Suns Game
3. Go to Plumbers' Association Trade Show in Las Vegas		
	1. Investigate vendors	
	2. Go to seminars	
		Stay a day afterward with wife and have fun

do it? I set a goal, focus on that goal and only that goal, and promise myself a reward when I hit that goal. (Notice I did not say *if*.)

The watch I wear right now is a gift I gave myself for bringing fifty people to a boot camp in the year 2000. It was my reward for hitting my goal. Every time I look to see what time it is, I am reminded of the success of my hard work that year. Now you might say a semi-wealthy individual like myself is hardly motivated by little gifts like this, but I really am. I like the competition and playing the game. Those of you who have seen my talks know I firmly believe that little things make a big difference. A little thing I like to do is take a picture of the gift I want for achieving something with that clear and specific goal written below it. I then place that picture on the wall near the door to my office at Grunder Landscaping, my office at home, on the dashboard of my truck, and on the bathroom mirror. I even laminate one and put it in the shower with me. Every time I see it, I'm reminded of what my goal is and what my reward will be if I achieve it. So I stay focused!

It's very important, folks, to reward yourself for achieving goals that are hard to achieve. If you don't reward yourself along the way toward a big goal, you won't make it. This works even for non-business goals. If you're trying to get in better shape, reward yourself on Sundays by eating a few treats. If you're trying to save money to buy a particular car, reward yourself with a small little prize when you save up part of the money for your car. This is an easy way to keep yourself focused on what your goal is. Especially big goals.

However, there are other rewards much simpler than a gift. Sometimes I'll reward myself for achieving a goal with an afternoon off to go watch the horse races. Or when I'm really under a deadline, I may say, "As soon as I write up twelve quotes, I can have lunch." You'd be amazed at what thinking about getting a Turkey-

Lurkey sandwich from my favorite deli, The Upper Krust, can motivate me to do.

One of the best rewards is simply to sit down and reflect on what you've accomplished. I do this often by looking at pictures I've taken of my ventures through the years, or by reading letters my clients have sent me thanking me for changing their life. But my favorite thing of all to do is to say to myself, "I did a great job, and I have a lot to be proud of. Look at everything I have. Life sure is great!" Try this; it certainly helps me, and I know it will help you.

How can you reward yourself for reaching your goals in running your own business? Here's an example of exactly how I'd go about it:

Let's say your goal is to have your own plumbing company by May 1, 2003. The big reward you get your first day in business is a used (but good looking and spotless) Ford truck with CD player and toolboxes.

Smaller goals that will get you to your ultimate goal

I carry a spiral notebook with me every day to the office or on the road in my briefcase. In that notebook is every goal and thing I want to do before I die. Each night before I go to bed, I pull out the worn and tattered notebook and transfer what I'm going to do the next day onto my 3" by 5" card that fits in my Levenger pocket briefcase. Use this method, and you'll get things done.

As I said earlier, it's really important to be positive. I will expand on this in Chapter 6. But plain and simple, you have to believe in yourself. You need to speak in present terms. You need to say, "I am the leading salesperson in my multi-level marketing group. I am the best real estate salesperson in the world. I am the most successful fishing guide in Bozeman, Montana. I am this city's most skillful personal shopper. I own my own welding company." Whatever you do, set your goal in the present. Even though you're not there yet, recite to yourself as if you have hit your goal. That way your goal is firmly planted in your mind, and makes its way into your subconscious, and pretty soon you're achieving it. Never use the word "if," only "when." Saying "if" implies you think you might not be able to do it. Saying "when" says "I will do it."

Well, you're through three chapters so far. Keep on going! Don't stop here.

chapter four

Get Paid to Learn

"I'm an owl.
I hope to watch, to learn and be wise."

—General H. Norman Schwarzkopf

Getting paid to learn is a great concept. You're probably dying to read on. In fact, you're reading fast because you've got to see how in the world someone could possibly get paid to learn. Well, slow down, boys and girls. You might already be doing this; you just don't realize it. You might even be doing this very, very well.

Whether you are an established entrepreneur or an aspiring one, getting paid to learn is one of the biggest secrets of success. If you jump into your business feet first and try to learn on your own money, there's a very good chance that you'll go bankrupt. Sure, that's a great way to learn how to do things right, but there's a major problem with it.

First of all it's a very expensive way to learn. Mistakes in business cost a lot of money. Those who choose to jump in must hope and pray that one of these mistakes doesn't bankrupt them. But the most dangerous thing about jumping in without experience is the possibility of damage to your reputation. As the popular Head and Shoulders dandruff shampoo commercial goes, "You never get a second chance to make a good first impression." If you jump in not knowing what you're doing, you will undoubtedly make mistakes that will affect your reputation and potentially alienate clients to the point they will never come back. You tell me what business' foundation of success isn't repeat clients. Wal-Mart, Ford, Ore-Ida French fries? How about Jim's Towing down at the end of the street? All of those companies are based on repeat business. Your reputation is everything. Your reputation is like the roof on your house. If you start bashing away at the walls, which is the services and products you offer, the roof, or your reputation, eventually will be crashing down. And, like a home, a reputation takes a long time to build and can be devastated in one flick of the wrist.

I was paid to learn at a young age. I was thirteen years old, and really didn't know what I was doing other than I loved cutting grass and had a goal of making $5,000 the first year toward the $40,000 I would need to get through college. Cutting grass was my passion. So brother Rich and I hit the street looking for clients. We lived in the country twenty miles south of Dayton, Ohio. So the bike ride between houses was long. All our "neighbors" (in the country, the word "neighbor" is used loosely) had large lawns. We thought that cutting the grass was something they'd pay someone to do. But we quickly found out that our initial marketing assumptions had major flaws. Our neighbors, whom we thought would pay us to have fun in their yard, would not. They moved to the country because they liked to work outside and surely weren't going to pay two young guys to have fun in their lawns. So it was back to the drawing board.

My mom, an eighth-grade teacher, got home right after we did every day at about 3:30. The very next week I asked Mom to take

Rich and me to the copy shop so we could have a flyer made. We ran off fifty flyers with a picture of a mower and our tractor on it and a brief description of our services. The next afternoon Rich and I drove our tractor six miles to a wealthy area of town. You can't legally operate a motor vehicle on the road unless you're sixteen, but in Ohio a driver's license isn't needed to drive a tractor on the road. All you need is one of those orange, reflective triangles that designate your vehicle as a "slow-moving vehicle." We went to this area of town with nice lawns because there were people who had their lawns mowed by a service. We knew this because Rich and I had seen lawn-mowing services working here.

We knocked on seventeen doors that afternoon and sold four jobs on the condition that we would mow these homeowners' lawns with a very small mower. We thought prospects would be impressed with our tractor idling in their driveway. But they weren't; they were scared, actually. They "didn't want that big tractor rutting up their yard." As we drove the tractor back, I was giddy over making four sales, but my brother was a little less certain. Over the tractor's loud, diesel engine he asked me, "Marty, why did you tell those people that we could mow their lawns with a small mower? We don't have one." He wondered what we were going to do. Well, I've always been a rather resourceful person and knew we could figure this out. The next day I asked my mom to take Rich and me to Sears to look at lawn mowers. I had $75 in my pocket. On our way to Sears, we passed a garage sale. To my excitement, I saw a mower out front. "Stop, Mom!" I yelled.

"What is it?" she said, thinking something bad had happened.

"Back there at the garage sale. Rich, look, it's a real nice push mower. I wonder how much it is."

We walked briskly up to the mower, and Rich pulled the starter rope. It started on the first pull! The owner saw our interest in his old mower and began to approach us. I quickly took a twenty-dollar bill and a five from the $75 I'd brought in my wallet and put them in my back pocket.

"Hello, boys!" the middle-aged gentleman said. "Hi," I said. "I'm Marty Grunder, and this is my brother Rich. We're starting a business and need a push mower. How much do you want for this old, used mower?"

"Fifty dollars," he said, "It is used and ten years old, but it works great. I'm moving to North Carolina, and I don't need one where I'm going."

"Oh . . . fifty dollars?! Well, we don't have that much money," I said. "We have $25." I pulled it out of my pocket and said, "Mister, would you take that?"

My mom stood by speechless as she watched my negotiating. Rich chimed in, "We really need one, mister."

"If you two will cut my grass two times this month while I'm in North Carolina moving in, you can have it for $25," the kind man said.

"Deal," I said without hesitating. (Little did I know that lawn was a $50/cut yard. In the end this deal was a great one for both sides!)

We put the mower in Mom's trunk and went home. The next day Grunder Landscaping Company was born as Grunder Lawn Service, and our first day sales were $51 as Rich and I mowed three lawns.

In a week Rich and I learned a little about how to sell, negotiate, and cut grass. Gradually, we learned about billing, payroll, human resources, taxes, customer service, and more about selling.

We were having a ball—making money cutting lawns and, without question, getting paid to learn. This learning experience made several of my classes at Alter High School and then at the University of Dayton much more enlightening. I was learning how to run a business and being paid to do it.

Learn on Someone Else's Dime

Even better is going to an established company and letting *them* pay you to learn. Consider the story of Milano's Subs and Salads, which is a legendary sub shop in my city. If you're ever traveling through Dayton, I highly recommend stopping and getting one of their sandwiches. Milano's was founded by Ronald Woods in the 1970s. Dennis, the owner's brother, told me the story late one night while I was getting a sandwich. He knew he wanted to have his own sandwich shop, but he wasn't quite sure how to do it so he moved to Chicago. He went to work for the finest sub and sandwich maker in Chicago and learned how to bake the bread and what kind of meats to combine and what kind of spices and seasonings and cheeses to put on the sandwiches. After he felt he had learned enough there, he went to Atlantic City, New Jersey and worked for a year for a very fine sandwich maker over there. He found out how to bake the bread, what condiments and dressings to add, which cheeses to combine, how to chill and store the meat, and so on. He learned a lot about the business he had in mind with these two stints at fine sandwich makers. He then brought all of these ideas back to Dayton, Ohio. On Brown Street there in the 1970s, there was a company called NCR, the National Cash Register Corporation. Today, NCR is a six billion-dollar-a-year, worldwide company, but it wasn't that big then. Mr. Woods realized that these people had to eat lunch so he opened up a little wagon selling sandwiches to the employees of NCR out on the street in front of the plant. Soon, the sandwich wagon could no longer accommodate what was going on. He was losing too much business, so he built a restaurant. Today, there are two Milano's sub shops and anyone who lives in Dayton and doesn't know what a Milano's sub is must live under a rock.

This is a classic case of how to develop a business. Why should you learn on your own money and make mistakes that cost you money? You should learn on someone else's dime. That's the easiest way to do things. Not only is learning how to run your business from others easier, it is cheaper, and certainly much less frustrating. There are a lot of things involved in running a business that you'll learn easily from another outfit. And in the end you will increase your odds of having a successful entrepreneurial venture.

Tens of thousands of companies have been started as a result of someone honing their skills at another firm. Bill Gates started Microsoft because IBM ignored his idea. But Bill learned computers on IBM's payroll. Mike McCall started BASS products after leaving NCR Corporation because he saw an opportunity to do something that NCR wasn't doing, but people wanted and needed. He sells scanning equipment for retail inventory. He sells over 15 million dollars' worth annually and was a 1996 recipient of an Entrepreneur of the Year Award from Ernst & Young.

Charles Shipman Payson hauled sugar to the U.S. on freighters in the 1940s. He hauled sugar in liquid form because less tax is assessed on the liquid form of sugar. His freight carriers were constantly replacing tanks due to the corrosion caused by the sugar. Mr. Payson saw this as an opportunity and put two chemists to work. They eventually developed and patented stainless steel which was then used to make tanks to haul the sugar, saving the freight companies millions as the tanks lasted forever. Hauling liquid sugar made Mr. Payson a lot of money. But getting paid to learn enabled Payson to come up with stainless steel which made him more money than the liquid sugar business ever would. That's the great thing about working for someone else. You will constantly be coming across other things you can do to make money. It creates opportunities to learn while being paid.

Clay Mathile purchased the Iams Corporation in 1976 when its annual sales were $500,000. He was the only salesman at the time and thought he could make Iams into something. While getting paid to learn, Clay realized the opportunity that Iams had and bought it. His one year at General Motors and seven years with Campbell's Soup earlier had taught him many valuable lessons. He then turned Iams into a 950 million-dollar-per-year giant with recognizable brands such as Eukanuba. In 1999 he sold Iams to Procter & Gamble for over 2 billion dollars in cash! He was the only shareholder.

Mark Grunkemeyer started Buckeye Ecocare in 1983 after a seven-year stint at ChemLawn. Today, Mark's company enjoys annual sales of around 2 million dollars and is very profitable. He provides lawn care services to thousands of Dayton residents. By working for an established company, he was able to get started quickly, have a viable business, and avoid many common mistakes.

Why reinvent the wheel after you've picked your passion? Go find those who perform your passion the best and ask if you can help them. If your passion is clothing, go work for the best tailor in town. If your passion is real estate, go work for the best agency in town. You get the idea. The time you spend learning all the tricks of the trade from these stars will advance your career light years in the long run. Remember, time is a unique commodity. Unlike clothes, cars, homes, and money, it cannot be manufactured or expanded. So guard your time wisely, and be aware that you'll save literally years by going straight to the source of success and copying how they do things.

People Want to Help Others

You're probably saying, "But I just can't work for someone to learn all their secrets and leave. They won't let me work there." Well, you're wrong. I have found and proven that people are happy to help. It's human nature to teach. Most successful people aren't afraid of competition. In fact, they often relish it. It's also very rewarding to teach. Just ask any schoolteacher! And behind every successful person, there's someone, some place, sometime who took the time out of their day and week to help that person. My suggestion to you is to ask as follows: "Hello, my name is Joe Entrepreneur, and I've eaten at your restaurant so much, I have the menu memorized. I really like to cook—so much so that I think I'd like to run my own restaurant some day. If you give me a job here so I can learn, I'll work my tail off for you and give you energy and enthusiasm you'll be impressed with. I'll be an excellent employee."

Now what wise business owner wouldn't take that offer? I know at our landscaping company, we have great trouble finding young men and women who want to work and put their heart into what they're doing. We would welcome the person described above. It's a win-win situation. The business owner gets a great worker who will help and treat the place as if it were his own, and the new employee gets paid to learn.

Now that I have you convinced you need to get paid to learn, you probably have some other questions. Let's suppose you're a student. What should you do? As I mentioned earlier, I'm a strong advocate of a co-op or an internship. Colleges throughout the country have programs designed to help students get a job in the particular area or field they're interested in. Corporations and companies, including Grunder Landscaping, love to have college students working at their place, and you'll find this to be true all over. As I said in Chapter 2, most entrepreneurs love having a person around their company who has my first step to success in place—a passion. They've picked a passion and now they're trying to find a job in it. It's a natural fit. They need a good job, and your firm needs help. They'd like to learn more about the business so you hire them, and the young person, or older person, is now getting paid to learn. I strongly suggest that you do a co-op or an internship someday, or do your part for America and hire a young person looking for this experience.

Experience Is Worth a Lot!

Sometimes you may not get paid anything up front to learn, but you'll get deferred compensation later. One of the clients of my landscaping company has cashed in on this idea big time.

While in college this fellow sent a letter to a prominent, well-known billionaire. He said he would work for him in the summers for free. The billionaire took him up on his offer, and my client learned enough about business that today he is the CEO of a billion-dollar-a-year publicly traded organization. This client wanted me to change the title of this chapter to something other than "Get Paid to Learn." He said that too many people are hung up on the short term when they should look at the long term. The experience he received (working for nothing) from the billionaire was worth millions.

To this day my client brings college students in to his own company and pays them minimum wage. Many of the kids say, "But I can make more money landscaping." To which my client says, "That's fine." He says they still take the job with his firm because they realize how valuable experience is. That's what I want you to realize. Experience is worth a lot. You don't want to quit your present job until you are sure that all the pieces are in place to get started on your entrepreneurial venture. Everywhere you work, you'll learn. With a well thought out plan that is your passion, working on your entrepreneurial dream won't seem like work at all. Success is a marathon, not a sprint. Those who have the patience and foresight to realize this will reach their goal faster and in a more satisfying way than those who don't. In short, if you have a choice between being a bouncer in a bar that pays $15 per hour and being a customer service representative at a successful, progressive company in your passion that pays $8 per hour but you'll learn a ton and be challenged, pick the latter. The $7 per hour you'll sacrifice will be more than made up later. Admittedly, it takes a smart, focused, determined, and frugal person to do this, but it works. Just ask some successful people in your area what their opinion is and what they'd do if they were you.

As a side note, many network-marketing companies offer a great opportunity to practice business and to work during the day somewhere else. Nikken Magnets is a good one if you believe in magnetic therapy. They have an excellent reputation. I was skeptical at first, but now I believe. My mother-in-law uses their products, and my racehorses have demonstrated a terrific response to the magnetic blankets. Check out their website at www.nikken.com and judge for yourself. I know a number of people who have done quite well with Nikken.

Take Getting Paid to Learn Seriously

Getting paid to learn is an important concept. Entrepreneurs typically think of their idea as foolproof. In fact, it is quite easy to talk yourself into the brilliance of your own idea. Don't be so certain your idea is great; look for indisputable proof that your venture, and every angle you have on it will work. When you look at your entrepreneurial dream this way, you'll take getting paid to learn seriously. So get a job in the field that supports both your passion and your goal. And don't worry about the personality of the entrepreneur who's paying you to learn. In fact, if that entrepreneur is much different from you, that's great. You will learn the most by interacting with people who are the least like you. They are the ones who shake you up, challenge you, and force you to think!

chapter five

Surround Yourself with Winners

"Keep away from people who try to belittle your ambitions.
Small people always do that, but the really great make you feel
that you, too, can become great.

—Mark Twain

Of all the secrets I'll share with you, none is more important than this one. Without question this secret has made more men and women millionaires than anything, myself included.

In 1997, the Florida Marlins won the World Series when they weren't supposed to. Clearly, the Cleveland Indians had more talent on their team, but the Marlins were winners led by a winner of a manager Jim Leyland. He had a collection of role players and journeymen (in other words, few "marquee" players) who knew what a team could accomplish when everyone was on the same page. With few superstars Jim Leyland did a masterful job. He's one of those people who just wins no matter what he does or where he goes, and people who want to succeed want to be with Jim Leyland. This happens regularly in sports. The New England Patriots won the 2002 Super Bowl with a strong cast of winners proving my theory again. Look at Bill Parcells, Pat Riley, Phil Jackson, Lou Holtz, and Rick Pitino. Much traveled coaches. As they move from job to job, they figure out how to win, and some of the players continue to go with them. Players want to play for these winners and sacrifice money to do so. Winning is contagious.

For these same basic reasons, you need to surround yourself with winners, both at work and in your spare time. For starters, I've found winners study other winners. They are constantly in search of new and better ways to do things and go to others for help.

Think and Grow Rich by Napoleon Hill was a study commissioned by Andrew Carnegie in which the author looked at and interviewed more than five hundred millionaires all over the world to find out what they had in common that might be responsible for their success. He interviewed people like Henry Ford of the automobile fame, William Wrigley, Jr., chewing gum magnate, George Eastman of Eastman Kodak, Charles M. Schwab, King Gillette, John D. Rockefeller, Thomas Edison, Theodore Roosevelt, Wilbur Wright, from Dayton, Ohio, Woodrow Wilson, William Howard Taft, Dr. Alexander Graham Bell, the inventor of the telephone, John H. Patterson, from Dayton, Ohio, founder of National Cash Register Corporation, M.W. Woolworth, the retail genius, and U.S. Senator Jennings Randolph, among others. Those are a fraction of the hundreds of well-known Americans whose achievements both financial and otherwise showed that they knew how to succeed. What did Hill find out about **how** they accomplished this?

They all realized that other successful people who have done what you want to do can help you become successful. Why reinvent the wheel when someone else might be able to give it to you? You don't necessarily have to read a book, go to college, or spend years trying to research what the secret may be. Go out and ask other people what they've done and find out what makes them tick. That is the quickest and best way to succeed.

The Paul Allen Story

A guy named Paul Allen is one of the best examples of the power of surrounding yourself with winners.

In 1975 *Popular Electronics* featured Ed Roberts on the cover of their magazine. Who is Ed Roberts, you ask? Today he is a doctor specializing in internal medicine in rural Georgia. He was also the inventor of the first personal computer—the MITS Altair 8800. In 1974 Roberts was busy trying to get this computer idea off the ground. For quite a while, he couldn't find one person who thought it was a good idea. Guess who rushed to Dr. Roberts's home in Albuquerque, New Mexico? Paul Allen did. At the time Paul Allen was Bill Gates' partner. Part of what Paul learned from Ed Roberts helped him get Microsoft off the ground.

In an *Inc.* magazine interview, Roberts had this to say about how he inadvertently helped launch Microsoft. He had spread the word that he would award a contract to the first person to bring him BASIC programming language for the Altair. "The first person who showed up was Paul Allen, and I hired him," Roberts recalls. "Paul impressed me then and still impresses me. I didn't meet Bill Gates for another six or seven months." Can you believe that? No one bothered to listen or to seek out Mr. Roberts. He was a winner and still is.

Once you've identified some winners, you need to dig deeply and almost pry into their past. These winners are winners for a reason. Study what they did before they became winners. This will lend insight into what you need to do on your own path to success. Take Clay Mathile, for example. He didn't wake up one day and become successful. He took a long, methodical path to success. Today Clay's foundation, The Center for Entrepreneurial Education, helps other entrepreneurs realize their fullest potential by focusing on what made Iams Corporation worth 2.3 billion to Procter & Gamble. I have taken advantage of his school. To my amazement, however, not near as many people seek out his center's help as you'd expect. Is it laziness or a lack of confidence or both?

My Own Winner's Circle

When I was growing up, my friends were all winners, people who helped me become successful. My friend Todd Romer is not just a great businessman but a great friend, father, and husband. He worked very hard to get through school. As the son of a physician, his family was well off and could afford many of the things other families couldn't. But Todd's dad and mom always made him work for what he needed, which was a great lesson that Todd will pass down on to his children, I'm sure. Todd served as a constant source of motivation to me through my teen and early adult years. Even today, his actions motivate me. When we were teenagers, he mowed over thirty lawns a week even though he didn't have to, to help pay for school and to have spending money through high school and college. Todd wanted to make money, and he is a winner that I'm happy to know and interact with.

John Schuermann is another good friend I've been fortunate enough to be around a lot. He's vice president of a major bank and has advanced as far as someone his age could. Never once has John ever shot down any dream I've had. If anything, he's thought that I didn't think big enough. His positive approach to life always makes me push on. I'm confident that one day John Schuermann will run that bank. He insists he has never read *How to Win Friends and Influence People*. But he's mastered the skills taught by Carnegie in the book. When he sees you, he smiles—always. He is an excellent listener and quickly looks for the easiest and most efficient way to do anything. In college he would listen intently in class and take concise but well detailed notes. As a result he received mostly A's without spending half the time the rest of us did. He has carried his skills to his job as a banker. And his ability to meet people, make friends, and spend time efficiently has enabled him to rapidly climb the ranks in his profession. His skills as a scratch golfer have been used to develop much new business on the golf course.

Bill Uhl, Jr., was a member of the University of Dayton Flyers basketball team that went to the third round of the NCAA tournament in 1990. At 6' 9" Bill is the biggest friend I've got. Today, he's president of the wildly successful Uhl Agency. The Uhl Agency insures thousands of Daytonians' homes, businesses, and lives. They hold onto clients like fly tape holds onto flies. I've always admired Bill for his modesty and his calm, collected approach. His patience has made him successful because he never loses his cool. He also is a tremendous father and husband.

The last winner that I hung around with growing up was John Brogan. He has influenced me more than anyone. He probably doesn't realize how much so. A fiercely competitive person who is fun to be around, John is a money manager in Chicago. He gets up most days, including weekends, at 6:00 a.m. to work out and often works eighty-plus hours a week! It's not uncommon for John to be in ten cities in a week. He is about the hardest working person I know. To this day I find myself pushing myself to beat John, which I think is healthy. The only things I am better at than John are baseball and landscaping, although he'd probably tell you he's better at everything!

You may be wondering why I've been rambling for so long about my friends. Why would I devote so much space in this book to that? Who cares? The reason is I want to show you how important it is to surround yourself with winners in your free time. The wrong kind of peer pressure is a vicious and damaging thing. It takes real courage and strength to be a success if all your friends choose to be lazy, make bad choices, and blame others for their failures and inadequacies. But the right kind of peer pressure is a great motivator. I graduated 153rd out of over 313 in my high school class, and with a 2.3 grade point average from the University of Dayton in Business Management. If success were determined solely by grades, I'd be nowhere. Luckily, my aforementioned friends were pushing themselves to succeed, and in them I saw some people I wanted to keep up with. I certainly didn't want to be the one who came home during the summer and said, "Well, I don't have a job yet." I saw that and gradually grew to believe that I had to be successful because everyone else was.

Another winner I spend time with is Dr. Stephen Levitt, a dermatologist and entrepreneur. He was one of my first clients and still is one today. "D.L.," as I call him, has been a friend and mentor for almost twenty years. I've learned a great deal from Steve. He showed me how to meet people and how to keep in touch with them. You may think that is a simple thing, but when you're sixteen, you don't know how to do that. He took the time to teach me this and many other lessons. He literally said, "Watch me as I walk up to this friend of mine and introduce you. Next time, you'll know how to do it." Learning how to do that while still a teenager was a terrific lesson. To this day I have lunch or dinner with Steve several times a year, and I always leave those meetings feeling great and ready to take on the world. He is a tremendous motivator.

The Lunch Or Breakfast Investment

I'm always looking for winners to spend time with. If I meet someone at a chamber function, political fundraiser, party, or other gathering, I send them a handwritten note with some information on my company. If the person really impressed me, I say in my note that I'd like to have breakfast or lunch with them. A couple of weeks later I call them personally and ask if I can have breakfast or lunch with them. (I have to eat, so I might as well make it productive.) The $15 or $20 I spend on breakfast or lunch is one of the best investments I make. It has enabled me to build one of Dayton, Ohio's most impressive networks of friends and winners. This network has not only taught me a ton, but generated millions of dollars worth of landscaping work.

Take a few minutes now and list three or four people in your city *you* would like to meet for lunch or breakfast. In the next two weeks, set up lunch or breakfast with each of them. By the way, breakfast is a great, cheap way to pull this off. Many people have only a cup of coffee. So if your budget is small, choose breakfast. Also, many very successful people get up early, and this might be your only shot at meeting with them. I feel better myself when I get up early and get the day started like this.

Without question this little secret has elevated my capabilities as an entrepreneur, father, husband, and friend. The logic of surrounding yourself with winners is simple but sound, if not brilliant. Not only is it motivational to talk regularly with successful people, it is tremendously educational. If you choose to go through life and business without consulting with others as you go, it will be difficult to reach the top. Conferring with others will help you improve your skills and avoid costly mistakes. Sometimes mind-boggling results can occur from seeking out, finding, and surrounding your-self with winners.

Look for "Outside Help" Too

You will never be the best if you look for help inside your industry only. You need to analyze other businesses and people for ideas to get your venture off the ground. I have toured grocery stores, city government offices, tool and die shops, and car dealerships, just to name a few. A lot of the processes and systems Grunder Land-scaping Company uses have come from other winning businesses. Business is business, as they say. The products and services may be different, but the goal is to make clients happy and make money. Several years ago I was hired to speak in Hilton Head, South Car-

reality check

Being observant is a great trait to have. For example, if you want to start your own plumbing company, start watching for plumbers' trucks. What neighborhoods are they working in? Whose trucks do you see the most? How many are in the yellow pages? Only small clues to success will be uncovered, but every clue helps. I've made a fortune from being observant not only in my town but in other towns and in other industries as well. There are processes, marketing ideas, and techniques that L. L. Bean, your church, and the local dry cleaners use that you can borrow and use in your business. Every time you see an idea, ask yourself "Could I use that idea in my venture? How?" And then go use those ideas.

olina, to the finance team of a publicly traded company. I was there for the whole weekend, and the CFO said if I were interested, I could sit in on their meeting. Needless to say, I said yes and learned so much in that three-hour period I should have paid them to speak. All of their problems were similar to my company's. They had receivable problems, inventory problems, and human resource challenges just like Grunder Landscaping did. But their solutions were so well thought out and effective, I couldn't wait to get back to try them. You too will find it very beneficial to study businesses and people both in your line of work and outside.

Be a Pirate!

In my talks I frequently define myself as "one of the world's greatest pirates." I then go on to explain how much money I've made surrounding myself with winners and searching out new ideas. Don't be afraid to borrow ideas, improve them, and adapt them for use in your own venture. Some ideas are copyrighted and thus cannot be legally copied. But most ideas and philosophies are up for grabs People claim to be the originator of a process, an idea, a quote, or even a joke. But few things like this are traceable back to someone specific. So don't feel bad about copying someone's idea or process. If it's not legally protected, it's fair game.

Here are two examples. The ballpoint pen was the inspiration behind roll-on deodorant. FedEx's system for package delivery was inspired by the Federal Reserve's check clearing process. There are many, many other cases where being an observant consumer has led to entrepreneurial fortunes being made.

Now an example from my own business. I was reading through a real estate magazine once when I came across a story on a product

101

called the Talking House. The Talking House (www.talking-house.com) is a nifty little transmitter that real estate salespeople use to pitch houses. The transmitter transmits a recorded message on AM radio. Signs placed in the yard of the house for sale direct you to tune your radio to a particular frequency. Once there, listeners hear all the details about the house. This is a very effective marketing tool. The minute I saw it, I immediately asked, "Could I use this idea in my business?" The answer was yes.

When you visit my landscaping company, you are greeted by a sign that says to tune your radio to AM 1610 for a special message from Grunder Landscaping Company. Once there, you'll hear a welcome message for all visitors. It is a nice touch and impresses most.

Find a Mentor

Now that I've given you an idea of how surrounding yourself with winners works, how can you do it?

When you attend one of the business boot camps I put on (notice I said when, not if), you'll be instructed to find a mentor. A business mentor is someone you can regularly rely on for all types of advice. Basically, a mentor is a coach, someone who has skills or knowledge in an area you are lacking. They have agreed to coach you in their area of expertise. I've had a number of mentors over the years. One is a very successful landscaper in Chicago. Another is Dottie Walters, the first lady of public speaking.

Don't Be Afraid to Ask!

A client and friend of mine is Bob Weerts, president of Weerts Companies in Winnebago, Minnesota. They are a multimillion-dollar holding company with interests in real estate, trucking, landscaping, and corn ethanol. At one of my boot camps, Bob heard me plead with the attendees to form a board of advisors and get a mentor. Bob was going to a pricey benefit dinner the Monday immediately after the boot camp. He asked me if I thought he should ask Glen Taylor, CEO of Taylor Corporation and owner of the Minnesota Timberwolves, to sit on his board of advisors. "Sure," I said, "what have you got to lose?"

So Bob attended the crowded, ritzy dinner and struck up a conversation with Mr. Taylor. He asked him if he would be interested in sitting on his board of advisors. Mr. Taylor said that he couldn't do that but to call his office, and he would "hook Bob up with his CFO" who would be happy to help him. The very next morning at 6:30 a.m., the phone at my desk rang. I rarely answer that phone myself, but I rarely get calls at 6:30 a.m., either. Curious, I answered the phone, and Bob went on to tell me the whole story. By just asking, Bob Weerts surrounded himself with one heck of a winner. Judging by the fact that this gentleman said yes to Bob's request so quickly, not many people have asked him for his help.

I'm a fairly successful guy and yet asked to sit on few boards. I often think it is because most people think I wouldn't say yes or are embarrassed to ask for help. Truth is, I'd love to help a local business. And most entrepreneurs feel the same way.

Make a Mastermind Group

"Mastermind groups" were groups that Napoleon Hill commanded his readers to join by seeking out people who have goals and values of the same or greater quantity and quality as you have. Once this mastermind group is formed, you meet biweekly or monthly to vocalize your progress toward your goal, the thought being that every member of the group can help motivate and educate the others to hit their goals.

Motivational speaker Mark Victor Hansen has taken this even one step further. Several years ago at an event Mark Victor shared the stage with Tony Robbins, the most successful person to date in the motivational business. He is to motivation what Microsoft is to computers. As Tony finished up, Mark approached him and said, "Tony, I've been doing this a long time and I'm doing okay. I'm making about a million dollars a year doing what I'm doing. I know for a fact that you made 156 million last year with your speaking and teaching and all of your products. How do you do it? How can I do it?"

Tony turned to him and asked, "Who's in your mastermind group?" "Millionaires," said Mark Victor, "we're all millionaires." And Tony said, "That's what you're doing wrong. You need to find yourself some billionaires and begin associating with them! They'll get you thinking at their level."

And that was the secret that Mark needed to turn his "Chicken Soup for the Soul" books and his company into the huge financial dynamo that they are today. It's important to surround yourself with winners who have ideas of the same quality and quantity as yours, but it's probably even more important to find people who have done far better at what you plan on doing than maybe you ever dreamed of. Because those are the people who will unlock all of the real secrets of what you want to do.

Once I started surrounding myself with winners who were way ahead of me, I was able to take Grunder Landscaping Company from $300,000 to 2.5 million a year at the time I'm writing this book. I fully believe and expect it will be a 5, 6, 7, 8, 9, and 10 milliondollar corporation someday.

"IT IS A PARADOXICAL BUT PROFOUNDLY TRUE
AND IMPORTANT PRINCIPLE OF LIFE
THAT THE MOST LIKELY WAY
TO REACH A GOAL
IS TO BE AIMING
NOT AT THAT GOAL ITSELF
BUT AT SOME MORE AMBITIOUS
GOAL BEYOND IT."

—Arnold Toynbee, economist, reformer

I regularly visit with the owners and managers of landscaping companies much more successful than mine. Frank Mariani is the founder and president of Mariani Landscape in Lake Bluff, Illinois. Mariani is a 20+ million-dollar-a-year firm. Several of our systems are an exact replica of his. We use the same schedule board they do and our prototype dump truck is a copy of theirs as well. Both items were improved to fit our needs. Steve Pattie is the founder and chairman of The Pattie Group in Cleveland, Ohio. His firm is arguably Ohio's best landscaping company. Steve has given me several ideas and models to use for improving my own company. Mike Rorie is the CEO and president of Groundmasters in Cincinnati, Ohio. They are a fast-growing landscape maintenance contractor with sales nearing 10 million. I regularly call Mike and eat lunch with him to get ideas and be inspired.

Why do I spend so much time with these people? For two reasons. One, time is precious, from both a financial and philosophical standpoint. From a financial perspective, time is money and the more time it takes for me to experiment doing certain tasks, the less time I can spend selling landscapes or traveling the U.S. and beyond speaking, both of which make me a nice amount of money. On the other hand, I (and you for that matter) only have so much time on this earth, so we want to make the most of it and not waste it! No matter how much money you have, you can't buy time. I have a great wife, Lisa, three terrific daughters, Emily, Kathleen, and Lillian, and a son, Grant, and I want to spend as much time with them as possible. Therefore, the less experimenting I do, the less time I waste while doing my work, the more time I will have available to spend with my family! I have a large ego, but not so large that I can't be humble enough to use someone else's idea. Think about it. Why waste time and money trying things? Go to a source of success and copy it!

Share Your Success with Others

The majority of ideas we use at Grunder Landscaping Company or Marty Grunder! Inc. have their roots in another company or person. We have repeatedly taken ideas, improved them, implemented them, and then shared them with others. Remember, do unto others as they've done to you. In other words, share your success and ideas with others. I've dedicated an entire two-and-a-half day boot camp to sharing ideas! I brought in successful people from all types of industries to share their best practices, and all attendees were required to share two ideas once they arrived at the camp.

Now that I'm growing my speaking and consulting business, I've sought out the leaders in that industry to talk with as well. We trade e-mails, notes, and ideas, and to your surprise not mine, of course, as I'm very confident, I've rubbed elbows with some of the best—Dale Dauten, Harvey Mackay, Tony Robbins, President Gerald Ford, Dan Kennedy, Zig Ziglar, and the list goes on and on. How? Just by asking. And you can do the same. Just ask for help. It is human nature to want to help.

Many heads working on an idea is better than one, and these are no ordinary heads! The more successful people you seek out, socialize with, and ask for feedback, the faster the ball gets rolling. The faster it rolls, the more pins it can knock down and so on. So go get your mastermind group and surround yourself with winners!

Expect Honesty If You Ask!

Just remember, when you ask for help, to expect honesty from those you're asking.

I heard Mark Victor Hansen tell the story one time of when the late Dr. Norman Vincent Peale and Dr. Ken Blanchard asked him to review a manuscript. Hansen vehemently disagreed with several points in their book and wrote them a twelve-page letter telling them how badly they had missed the boat. He became worried that he would even lose Dr. Peale and Dr. Blanchard's friendship and respect over his comments. But Hansen decided he needed to be honest and sent off the letter anyway. When they received it, Doctors Peale and Blanchard called Hansen back, thanked him for his frankness, and made changes accordingly so that the book could be successful. They were very grateful for his suggestions on how they could improve their work.

Similarly, when Hansen and Canfield were finalizing their first *Chicken Soup for the Soul* book, they sent it out to over one hundred people for critiques. They were looking for people to tell them what they thought of their book. They got a lot of great, positive feedback, but they got some very negative feedback as well, such as many did not care for them telling readers to call their moms. They said, "Just tell the story, Mark and Jack. Don't preach to us." Hence Hansen and Canfield made some changes.

Surrounding yourself with winners is a sure way to speed up success. Being comfortable and mature enough with those who are giving you their advice to ask them for their unbiased, honest opinions is a "sure-fire" way to put your endeavor over the top.

Now You Need a Network

Okay, we've talked about surrounding yourself with winners. We've talked about picking your friends wisely and the importance peer pressure plays in motivating yourself. We've talked about formulating your mastermind group and how important it is to surround yourself with winners, with people who have goals and ideas of at least the same quantity and quality as yours. I've even suggested you seek out people who have done way better than you are doing now or plan to do. Hopefully, you'll seek out people who have succeeded to the greatest level in the particular endeavor that you're pursuing, because those are the folks who will really unlock the secrets.

Now you need to develop a network, and I'm not talking about the kind of network that involves those computer cables that run through your office or your house. I'm talking about that large group of people who fit neither the category of your friends nor your mastermind group, but are just as important. It is your network that will help put your business or your endeavor into outer space. This is all of the acquaintances, clients, colleagues, prospects, and others you know who can either use the product or service you're offering, or who know people who could use it. Many times you've heard the cliché, "It's not what you know, but who you know." I've changed that because I've found that it's not what you know or who you know that matters the most here, but *who knows you.*

Think about that. *It's not what you know or who you know, but who knows you.* I'm not saying that what you know isn't important. The more you know about your product or service, the better off you'll be.

Brian Tracy, a masterful speaker, author, consultant, and coach, teaches that anyone can become an expert on something in a year by reading everything there is available on it. I think if you read as Tracy suggests and add surfing the web for info and companies that do what you do or want to do, watching TV, and going to seminars, you'll get there in less than a year. I think you can do it in eight months. The knowledge you gain will give you confidence, because as we discussed earlier, knowledge is confidence, and confidence enables people to conquer the world. Confident people succeed at a much higher rate than cowards. Look at professional athletes. Look how confident some of those guys are to return a punt in the Super Bowl for a touchdown like Desmond Howard did a few years ago. So, please, don't go sending me notes or e-mails saying that I said what you know isn't important. It's critical, but it's not the only thing.

I'm not saying that who you know isn't important, either. My speaking colleague, Harvey Mackay, has mastered this part of the equation better than anyone I know. They should change his middle name to "Rolodex." Heck, he probably invented the Rolodex. He knows everyone. This talent Harvey has for meeting people is something you need to develop. He knows people who can help him do just about anything. Politicians typically are very good at meeting people and finding people to help them. That's how they got elected. So are very successful entrepreneurs. They're terrific delegators.

But the really good ones perfect the last part of my cliché, that business of "who knows you." Who knows you is more important than what you know or who you know. Why? Because it really doesn't matter what you know or who you know if, when a person needs your product or service, they don't think of you. That's why an effective marketing plan is essential to the success of your venture. You must have a target audience—people who either need or know people who need your product or service. This is called target or smart bomb marketing. The term "smart bomb" became familiar in the Persian Gulf War of 1990. I was glued to the TV then as a college senior, watching these bombs being fired from miles away and hitting targets as small as an office. Smart bomb marketing means marketing that knows its target. All of your marketing should have a clear and specific target. For example, if your entrepreneurial venture is an upscale, ritzy restaurant, it makes no sense to mail your grand opening announcement to a ZIP code that has an average household income of $15,000 or less. If you were opening a Subway sandwich shop, on the other hand, marketing to this income level is probably a great idea as just about everyone would be a good target for a sandwich shop. Your grand opening announcement for your ritzy restaurant should go to all Mercedes-Benz, BMW, and Porsche owners in that area. This information is attainable. I know because I get offers centered around the fact I drive an SUV (sports utility vehicle) . Not a month goes by that I don't get some type of camping magazine, SUV accessory, or outdoors catalog. You can find the people you're after. You just have to look hard and work hard. Look in the business yellow pages under mailing lists, and you will find several companies that can help you target your marketing, or visit www.usps.com, the Postal Service's website. There are some tools there that can help you.

In one of my business courses at the University of Dayton, the professor stressed over and over that the average consumer must see a name twenty-seven times until they will recall it in their time of need. In other words, someone must see your name more than two dozen times on average before they associate your name with what you do. Getting our name out is something Grunder Landscaping Company has done very well in Dayton, Ohio. We're one of the most recognizable names in landscaping in Dayton, and we're a relatively young company. So get to work now surrounding yourself with people who can or who know people who can use your products or services.

Ways To Build Or Expand a Network

There are several ways you can do this. Some easy and cheap, some difficult, some expensive, and some even fun. Here are some simple steps you can take to greatly increase who knows you:

1. *Place your photo on marketing pieces.* Place a high-quality head and shoulders photo on your business cards, stationery, and all advertising. Graphic artists will tell you this looks bad. Ignore them. They may know graphics, they may know what looks pretty, and they may know what looks creative, but they don't know marketing. The goal is to get people to know who you are and what you do so well they remember you when they need you. Your picture on your business card, your letterhead, in any ads you run, and any other appropriate place will help poten-

tial clients (the people you're trying to get to know you) remember you when they need you. Then pass those cards out everywhere. This small step says, "I'm a friendly person who wants to meet and help you."

Because my picture has been on our newsletter for years, people I don't know frequently say "Hi, Marty" to me. When I say, "I'm sorry; I can't remember your name," they reply, "Oh, we've never met, but I get your newsletter and have seen your picture in the paper." This can and will happen to you if you use this valuable tip.

2. *Write articles or columns and submit them.* The second way you can draw attention to yourself and improve your network of people is to write articles, or even a regular column for a local newspaper. It doesn't matter how big or small the paper is. Your picture and your name in print give you instant credibility. Furthermore, those articles can then be copied (get permission if necessary) or reprinted and used as part of your other marketing endeavors to build credibility. Trade magazines and newsletters, too, are always in need of fresh topics. I have written or appeared in more than seventy-five different stories in various magazines, papers, websites, etc., using this technique.

3. *Volunteer.* Basically, this means get involved. You'll feel good because you're helping people, and you'll broaden your network. Any association you join, you should be an active member of. That's the only way you'll benefit. If I can't get involved, I won't join.

There are many groups and organizations around that can help you meet people who can use your goods or services or who know people who need them. These include parent-teacher associations or PTA, church groups, neighborhood associations, and women's auxiliaries. Ask people in your area what the groups and volunteer opportunities are and investigate. You could chair the golf outing, for instance, at your local Optimists, Rotary, or chamber organization. It's a very simple way to get your name out and have everyone know who you are. Heck, do the keynote address at the dinner after the outing. By the time you're done, everyone will know who you are.

4. *Be someone others want to be around.* Probably the most important way you can network with people is to just be a positive person. Approach people, and be someone they want to be around. It's okay to be funny. Don't be too funny. It's okay to be interested in someone. Don't be over-interested. Smile when people look at you. Listen to people when they talk to you. Be positive (I know I mentioned

reality check

If you were a deer hunter, would you take your shotgun into the city looking for deer? The answer is no. Not only could you get arrested, but you would not find any deer. Marketing is no different. Aim your message to those you want as clients, and to a place where they are likely to be and fire away!

positive two times), be supportive of others, and help them. Do these things, and others will help you. I strongly recommend that you read Dale Carnegie's *How to Win Friends and Influence People*. It's a terrific book that will teach you how to take an interest in people, and thereby they'll take an interest in you.

5. *Speak to groups*. Another way you can create interest in yourself and network is to give talks. If you happen to be a local real estate agent, give a talk to the Optimist and Rotary clubs in your area about the ten things you can do to your house to get the best price for it at sale time. If you're involved in Amway or Usana or any of the multi-level marketing companies, put a talk together that centers on why it's a great idea to get involved with those types of things. If you sell vitamins for Shaklee, give a talk on the power of vitamins in our overall health and well-being. For years I spoke to groups everywhere. My landscaping company benefited, and my self-confidence and presentation skills grew tremendously. But most of all, those little talks turned into big talks. Today I speak to thousands each month. I never would have realized this unless I started speaking. Another case of "the harder you work, the luckier you get" and getting paid to learn.

6. *Send notes*. One of the neatest ways I've found to build rapport with people and network well is to get personalized 3" x 5" cards made up with your name on them that fit in the Levenger pocket briefcase I mentioned earlier in the book. On these, I hand write many notes. It takes very little

time, and people really warm to a handwritten thank you or informational note. Read on for another way to use notes.

7. *Send clippings.* I read many periodicals on a weekly and daily basis. When I come across an article I know a client or prospect may be interested in, I cut it out. Then I drop it in the mail along with a note that says, "Hello, George. Thought you might like reading this article. Hope you're doing great. Keep in touch. Marty." This is a great way to keep in touch with clients and prospects. I learned this little technique from my friend and client Andy Furman of WLW-AM 700 in Cincinnati, Ohio. Andy is host of one of the top-ranked radio sports talk shows in the country. Not long ago he signed a multimillion-dollar contract to stay on the show! He reads hundreds of publications every month. While reading he cuts out any article that might be of interest to someone he knows. On average, I receive six to ten notes a year from Andy with articles on everything from landscaping and public speaking to horse racing and my beloved UD Flyers. Needless to say, Andy's efforts to stay in touch with people enable him to call in many favors. He often interviews big sports stars because he keeps in touch with them like this. As a result, many people know who Andy is. He hardly goes anywhere in Cincinnati where people don't say "hi"! If he were on television, you'd expect people to know who he is. But since he's on the radio, the fact people recognize him is a testament to his networking talents. And his show's success is due in large part to Andy's efforts to make sure people know who he is!

8. *Teach*. Another way that you can network is to teach a class. If you happen to own a local restaurant, it might make sense to teach a class in cooking. Sure, you may give away a couple of secrets, but you also might create a great deal of interest in your restaurant just in the students that you have in the class (and their friends and relatives). You may even find a few great new team members.

Please go over the above list again. Notice that none of these ideas cost much, so there should be no reason you can't do them.

You can never have too many friends and acquaintances. It's absolutely impossible. Friends can help you in business and can help you when you need them. Just remember that here, too, it's important to target your efforts to people who can use your product or service. If you are trying to get a home remodeling business off the ground, it makes no sense to do a mailing to apartment owners. Better to speak at the local Rotary club, where a high percentage of the attendees will be homeowners.

The Wonders of Word-of-Mouth

Again, it's not what you know or who you know, but who knows you. If the right group of people knows you, your message will be heard and spread, and there is **nothing** more powerful in business than word-of-mouth advertising! I learned this at a very young age. When I was about six, I started to notice dump trucks going by my parent's house on their way to a nearby gravel pit. Many of the trucks had a name on the side. The nicest truck had the name "Roy Haines Trucking" on the side. When we needed gravel for our driveway, guess who I told my dad to call? Dad said, "Where did you hear about this Roy Haines Trucking?" "From the sign on their truck," I answered. My dad could only chuckle at my observation. I loved trucks then, and I still do. And I promised my brother that when we had our first truck, we'd get a nice sign that read "Grunder Lawn Service." At age sixteen I proudly posed for a picture with my brother Rich in front of Dad's truck that he let us use with a new sign that read "Grunder Lawn Service"!! We sold so much work from that sign that to this day we letter every truck, trailer, and piece of equipment we have because signs are without question the best dollar-for-dollar advertising you can do in any industry. You pay for the sign once, and it keeps on giving and giving. Uniforms, license plate brackets, pens, coffee cups, and even hot air balloons are all excellent, effective forms of advertising. The point is to get your name out there and constantly be searching for winners who can help you either by giving you advice or by purchasing your product or service.

chapter six

Believe in Yourself

"Once you say you're going to settle for second, that's what happens to you in life, I find."

—President John F. Kennedy

Do you know what the most common fear amongst Americans today is? This fear is even greater than fear of dying or fear of failure. It is the fear of public speaking. That is what most people say their biggest fear in life is.

Think about the last time *you* were asked to get up in front of a group of people and talk. It's kind of an unnerving experience, isn't it? I address thousands of people every year—some of my audiences are as large as 10,000 people. But I'm not afraid of speaking in front of groups, small or large. Why is that? Because I believe in myself.

Psychologists have studied this deeply. They found that some people are not afraid of speaking in front of others because they believe in themselves. They also believe in what they are going to say, and have confidence that they can get up there and do the job that needs to be done. People who are afraid of public speaking, on the other hand, don't believe in themselves. They don't want to get up and say anything because they're afraid someone might laugh at them for taking another side of an opinion—for saying something that might be different from what everyone has heard before. They're afraid that maybe their idea is silly. They're afraid that maybe their idea won't work. I've found many aspiring entrepreneurs lack confidence too. And yet confidence is absolutely necessary to succeed.

I used to lack confidence and I used to be extremely intimidated to speak in front of people. I felt, "Who in the world wants to hear what I have to say? I have a little million-dollar-a-year landscaping company in the middle of Ohio. Why do they care what I have to say? Look at people like Michael Dell of Dell Computers who's worth several billion dollars. Let's listen to what he has to say. Let's listen to Bill Gates. What does he have to say? Let's listen to Joe Torre, manager of the New York Yankees. Let's listen to Elizabeth Dole, one of the brightest women alive. Let's listen to Phil Jackson, winner of nine NBA world championships. No one wants to listen to Marty Grunder; he has a very simple story to tell."

That's what I thought the first time I spoke in public. I remember my first presentation like it was yesterday. I was asked to tell my story to a group of aspiring entrepreneurs in October 1993. I was so nervous my heels were pulsating, and I felt like I was rocking back and forth like one of those old-fashioned toy mercury birds. My mouth felt like someone had poured cement in it, and no matter how much water I drank, my tongue remained dry, and my voice cracked like I was going through puberty again. I was sweating profusely. But as I got started and went along, the audience laughed—with me, not at me. A mature African-American man in the front row said "awesome" at various points in my talk. That man must have been a genius—he gave me just the dose of confidence I needed. My tongue suddenly became normal, I quit shaking,

119

and really got on a roll. I ended my first talk using one of the same lines I use today, "Thanks, and remember—the harder you work, the luckier you get." The audience gave me a standing ovation! I couldn't believe it. I did it again about a month later and got another rousing response. Then I did it again. And again. Soon someone asked me, "Well, how much do you charge to give your talk?" I quickly yet nervously responded, "Four hundred dollars is what I charge," even though I'd never charged for a talk before. They said, "That's fine. We'd like for you to speak to our group of insurance agents next month." And then I went on to do it. Pretty soon I realized that, yes, my story is simple, but how many people in any given audience have ever cut grass to make money? Answer—a lot. How many people in any given audience have a goal and a dream and wake up every day and try to chase that dream or goal? A great many of them. People also love to hear success stories. It's human nature. I love to hear success stories. I love to hear about teachers who go into inner city schools and turn things around. I love to hear about the undrafted rookie free agent who makes the football team and ends up being an all-pro. I love to hear about the horse that was purchased for $17,000, like Real Quiet, who goes on to win the Kentucky Derby. Mine was a success story, too, so I began to believe I could get up in front of people and tell them what I have done. I had a story that could help people. I could change some lives. I could teach some people. I could help them make better use of their time and go on to be something truly spectacular. And slowly my confidence grew and grew to the point that I believed in myself, and no one was going to deny me getting up in front of a group and doing my talk. I had a gift for speaking, and I was going to use it! That's the way you need to be.

Start Believing in Yourself **Now**

As we talk more about Step Number 5 in The Nine Super Simple Steps to Entrepreneurial Success, you must start now believing in yourself. Say to yourself now, "I have confidence that I can do what I have in mind and that it will go very well." Earl Nightingale, the legendary motivational speaker and writer, uncovered what he called the strangest secret years ago. He said, revealing his secret—"You are and you become what you think about."

You are and you become what you think about. Why don't we ponder that for a second? Basically, what that means is, if you think you're going to be a success, you will be. If you think that you're going to fail, you will. That boils down to positive thinking, doesn't it? Self-confidence is critical to your success. Without it you'll never make it. So use positive thinking to help you reach your goal. The body works better when the brain is full of positive thoughts. Positive people succeed regularly because they condition themselves to seeing the good and ignoring the bad. Positive people also lift up everyone around them. If you are positive, your team will catch on, and feel better about themselves! They will run through a wall for you and elevate their performances to their utmost potential.

My friend Jim O'Brien proved this in 1990 as the head basketball coach at the University of Dayton. He took a group of "underachievers" who played basketball, and in his first year as head basketball coach for the Flyers, turned their fortunes around so that they went to the Sweet 16 in the NCAA tournament. It should come as no surprise that O'Brien practiced Norman Vincent Peale's positive thought theory. Today, Jim is the head coach of the NBA's Boston Celtics.

Motivational speaker and football coach Lou Holtz signed on with the pitiful football team of the University of South Carolina to be their head coach in 1999. People asked why? But in 2000 he won the Outback Bowl over the bigger, faster, better Ohio State Buckeyes. But Lou Holtz wasn't always successful.

In 1976, Lou Holtz left collegiate sports and signed a five-year contract to coach the New York Jets. At this time, the New York Jets' head coaching job was one of the most sought-after coaching positions in all of pro football. The fans were extremely enthusiastic about Lou Holtz joining the team as head coach. The owner, the late Leon Hess, was also very supportive. Yet Holtz did not approach the job in the greatest frame of mind. He saw every problem as a defeat and another sign that things weren't really going to work out for him. In '76, the Jets went 3-10, and he quit only eight months into his contract. Why did he quit? Why did he give up? He realized that he'd gone into this job thinking that there was no way the Jets could win. He assumed that he would fail, that things would just not work out, and he proved himself right. But he had a chance to redeem himself.

Years later, Lou Holtz was asked by the Minnesota Golden Gophers to coach their football team. At first, he turned the job down. The team was not a good one. Other coaches around the country had no interest in it. And Holtz really wasn't too excited about coaching in the middle of a state like Minnesota, although I think Minnesota is beautiful. Finally, after persistent pressure from officials at the University of Minnesota, he started there in 1984. But this time when Lou Holtz decided he was going to be coaching a team, he decided he was going to win, and that if he took on this job, it would work. In his first season in 1984, Lou Holtz helped the

reality check

You're only as young or old as you act. Regardless of what anyone may tell you, how young or old you are has nothing to do whether or not you are successful. What matters is that your endeavor be well thought out and that you believe in it. Enthusiasm and confidence sell. They sell your idea to bankers for financing, to prospects for sales, and to potential employees for workers. Plain and simple, confidence matters most, not your age.

Gophers improve their game attendance to 54,000 per game, and in the second season the team went on to the Independence Bowl.

Lou Holtz realized that your motivation determines how much you're willing to do. Your attitude determines how well you do it. One of the things I remember him saying in a talk once was to never underestimate your assets and never overestimate another person's pluses. Don't compare yourself to anyone.

That is advice I have used throughout the years. I know there are a lot of things I can do. I'm working right now to become a nationally recognized motivational speaker and author, and there is not one bone in my body that doubts I can do this. This is what separates winners from losers. Winners believe in themselves. Winners believe that they can win. They think that they **will** do something. Do you think Mark McGwire went to the plate and said, "I think I can hit a single, or I might strike out"? No, Mark McGwire went to home plate saying, "I know I can hit a home run." When Mark McGwire and Sammy Sosa were in pursuit of Roger Maris' seemingly unbreakable 61 home runs in 1998, I am sure both of them knew that they could do it, and sure enough they both zoomed right on by 61. That's the difference between winning and losing.

If you think you are going to graduate from college, there's a good chance that you will. If you walk into a situation believing that you will fail, you will fail. That's what life's all about, folks. You have to have confidence in yourself, and you have to believe in your goal.

A Good Way To Build Confidence

One sure-fire way to help build confidence in your dream or your goal is to vocalize it to as many people as you can. It takes a tremendous amount of confidence to do this. You will possibly be labeled "a braggart" by some. But other successful people will know what you're doing and support you. For years, I told people when I did a talk that I aspired to be a nationally recognized motivational speaker and author and that I was working on a book that someday will be published. And every time I said that, it was a little reminder to me that, gosh, I can't give up on my pursuit of my goal. Think about all the people I told I was going to do this. I could never let them down. I could never see them and say, you know, I never did get the book done, or I never did reach my goal of being a nationally recognized motivational speaker. It's extremely important that you believe in yourself.

Five Tons of Confidence

Enrolling in school in August 1986, I also bought my first new truck, a red 1986 Ford Ranger, which is green today, and still in the fleet, with 183,452.4 miles on it at last check. By December 1986, I still had the nice red Ford Ranger, but I had a grade point average of 1.8.

For those of you unfamiliar with grade point averages, that means you're getting several F's and a couple D's for fun. And "D," in this case, did not stand for "diploma." "D" stood for disaster. I was going to work to get away from school, and my grades showed that to be the case. But I really believed in myself and my business, and I knew I should be doing better in school.

The business was thriving. Whereas my friends always had to ask their parents for a few dollars to get through the week, I never asked my parents for money. In fact, I haven't asked my parents for any money since the eighth grade. My parents, however, were thoroughly disgusted with me. Getting a 1.8 in a household in which your parents are both college graduates is not acceptable. My mom and dad were well educated and expected the same from their children. My grades were a real embarrassment, and I knew I needed to work on them. But I also knew I had a business that could turn into something. So I went to my mom and dad and said, "Mom, Dad, brother Rich and I want to buy a dump truck. We're tired of raking things off of flatbed trucks. Our backs hurt. We're going to have to go to the chiropractor soon. Heck, Mom and Dad, brother Rich might even have to have back surgery, that's how sore he is." (This of course was a story.)

Now that wasn't the only reason we wanted a dump truck, folks. While most eighteen-year-old men are interested in pretty girls, video games, CDs, and playing sports, not Marty Grunder. Marty Grunder was interested in a dump truck. Why? Well, because I'm a redneck. A sophisticated redneck, maybe, but still a redneck. And I was totally in love with heavy equipment and trucks, and I still am today. (There's that passion thing again.) One of the most enjoyable things I do for therapy is to get in one of our company's big dump trucks and take it out on a delivery run. I love the power that you have behind the wheel and the way people look up to you in those big trucks. Karl Malone, a future NBA Hall of Famer, has a big truck he drives for fun too!

I wanted and needed a dump truck and pleaded with my mom and dad to help me buy one as I didn't think I could get one on my own. My mom looked at my dad. My dad looked at my mom. My mom looked at my dad. And my dad looked at my mom. My mom, often being the one who would have to break the silence when I came up with another crazy idea, looked me right in the eye and said, "Marty, you're not getting any dump truck. What you need to do is get your butt back on down to school and get a diploma so that you don't end up an unemployed mechanic."

I said, "Mom, a mechanic, let alone an unemployed mechanic?" She said that was the end of the story, and I was not getting the dump truck because they weren't going to help me.

Well, at age eighteen, all Marty Grunder needed to be told was that he couldn't do something. At that age (and to this day), I was full of determination to reach my dream, and at this time my dream was a dump truck which literally was the key to my future. I sat up late that night and thought very hard about what could enable me to get this truck. I wanted the dump truck more than anything, anytime, anywhere.

I came up with the following plan: The dump truck I had found was for sale for $12,500. A landscaper was selling it. It was a nice blue truck with a ten-foot dump bed. I convinced the landscaper to sell the truck for $10,000, $2,500 less than what he was asking for it. Then I went to two of the clients I had at the time. They are still clients of mine today—Dr. Michael Ervin and Dr. Steven Levitt. Dr. Ervin was a pioneer in Dayton as he started the Aircare Emergency Response Team at Miami Valley Hospital. Dr. Levitt is one of the few doctors I've ever met who truly is a tremendous businessman. Dr. Levitt has six offices and keeps unbelievable hours, working from 3:30 in the morning until 6:00 at night, six days a week. Sundays he's in the office all day doing paperwork. He's really been an inspiration to me and today is a close friend and mentor. I went to both of these clients in 1987 and convinced them to prepay their contracts for the entire year, which was a total of $10,000. I was thrilled when Dr. Levitt spoke up, "I'll pay my half, and Mike will too."

They each gave me a check for $5,000. I took that $10,000 to the local small town bank, the Bellbrook Community Bank. The bank president at the time was John Gloyd, and I said, "Mr. Gloyd, here's $10,000 that I'm going to deposit in your fine financial institution. I want you to take $5,000 of this and deposit it into an operating account that I can use for working capital. I want to take the other $5,000 and use it as a down payment on a dump truck worth $12,500 that I have secured for a bid of $10,000. As I see it, Mr. Gloyd, if I would fail, and I can assure you right now that I have no intentions of failing, but let's just suppose—worst case scenario—that I do, and you have to take the dump truck back, you're going to get an asset back that is valued at $12,500, and your exposure is only $5,000. That would make for a pretty good investment should I fail. Dump trucks are easy to sell, and certainly you could get $11,000 or maybe even $12,500 for it a few months from now."

Mr. Gloyd looked at me, took off his glasses, and said, "Marty, you've obviously thought long and hard about this plan, and it sounds to me like this dump truck is something that you really want, and maybe you even really need it, but I can't make a decision like this right away. I must take it before the board."

Well, when Mr. Gloyd said this, I thought, "I know what that means. That probably means I'm not going to get the loan." And all I wanted was $5,000. I thought, "Gosh, that's probably in one of those drawers up there. There might even be that much money in the coffee fund." But, nonetheless, Mr. Gloyd literally held the key to my future in the form of this dump truck, so I did nothing other than to smile and say, "I appreciate your consideration, and I hope that you will give me the loan and start what surely will be one of Dayton's most respected businesses in years to come." I left the bank and made the twenty-minute drive back on down to the University of Dayton, went up to my room in Stuart Hall, and pondered about what my future would be like without this dump truck. It wouldn't be much, I thought. The dump truck surely was a way of my growing this business and hopefully realizing my dream. A week went by. Eight days went by. Nine days went by. And I still had no answer back from the bank. Needless to say, by this time, I was pretty sure I wasn't going to get the loan from the bank, and I'd have to figure out some other way.

There was one thing I did know, and that was I was going to get this dump truck some way, one way or another, whether the Bellbrook Community Bank was involved or not. Ten days had passed at this point. I went to the snack bar of Stuart Hall and got a cheeseburger (I love cheeseburgers). Then I got on the elevator, went up to the fifth floor of the dormitory, and went down five steps to the third door on the right. When I opened up my dorm room, which was approximately 12' x 20' (the whole room!), I saw that the light on my message machine was flashing. I thought, "Oh, somebody must want to go out and do something, have some fun, play basketball or something." But, much to my surprise, it was Mr. Gloyd from the bank. He said, "Marty, I need to talk to you. You need to come in to the bank" in a very solemn, somber tone.

Well, I knew what that meant, just by the tone of his voice. It was 2:00 in the afternoon and the way he was talking, I wasn't going to get the loan for my dump truck. So instead of jumping in my truck and driving to the bank to hear what he had to say, I decided to have a pity party. Pity parties are very lonely parties. Only one person comes to a pity party, and that's you. And I don't recommend them for anyone. But I had one heck of a pity party for the next three hours and five minutes. What otherwise was a twenty-minute drive to the bank from my dorm room turned into a three-hour drive all across Dayton feeling sorry for myself and wondering what in the world I was going to do now that Mr. Gloyd was going to tell me that I couldn't get my dump truck. I assumed that he'd say no. At five minutes after five, I walked into the bank. Mr. Gloyd stood there with his briefcase in hand and said, "Marty, come on in, I've been waiting for you for three hours. Where have you been?"

I said, "I've been busy, Mr. Gloyd, I'm sorry."

He said, "Well, have a seat. I have a question to ask you, Marty."

I said, "Yes, Mr. Gloyd?" He said, "Is your uncle's name John Grunder?"

I said, "Why, yes, sir, it is."

He said, "He's a very prominent banker in town, isn't he?"

And I said, "Yes, sir, he is."

He said, "He's with First National Bank, right?"

I said, "Yes, sir, he is."

He said, "Well, the board had a question last night when we took your request for a loan before a vote, and they wanted me to ask you why on earth, if your uncle was in that kind of a position, would you come up here and ask us for a loan when you know your uncle could get it done just like that?"

Well, I'd thought long and hard about this, and I was prepared, much the same as a lawyer prepares the defendant for cross-examination. I said, "Mr. Gloyd, it's very important to me that I do things on my own. I know full well I could walk into First National Bank, and my uncle would give me whatever amount of money I wanted just because he was my uncle, and he trusts me, but that's not what I want to do. I want to do this on my own. Years from now I want to be able to say that I bought this dump truck on my own, that I had no help, that it really was my dump truck, not my dad's dump truck, not my uncle's dump truck; it was through my own hard work that I got this truck."

Mr. Gloyd took his glasses off, paused for a moment, and then looked me in the eye and said, "Marty, I knew that's what you'd say. I could tell when I met with you ten days ago that that's the kind of person you are—you don't want to have someone to lean on. You want to do things yourself. That's why one day, young man, you're going to be very, very successful." He said, "That's what I told the board you'd say, and I am happy to say that last night the board voted unanimously to give you the $5,000 loan for the $10,000 dump truck that you say is worth $12,500, which we found out is absolutely correct."

Well, I nearly leapt over Mr. Gloyd's desk and gave him a hug and a kiss. I quickly composed myself, realized that would be most inappropriate, stood up, shook Mr. Gloyd's hand and said, "Thank you for doing business with my company, Mr. Gloyd. You'll be very glad you did. I really appreciate you giving us a chance. Have a great day."

The real reason I didn't ask my uncle for the money was simple. If I had asked Uncle John for $5,000 for the truck, he would have told my parents what I was scheming and who knows what steps my folks would have taken to stop me from buying a dump truck. School was what they wanted me to focus on, not dump trucks!

I ran out of the bank and jumped into my Ford Ranger, picked up the cellular phone I had purchased three weeks before for $1,500—this is 1986, and yes a cellular phone was $1,500 (today they give them to you)—and I called my brother who was at home, and I said, "Rich, I've got some great news for you. We've got ourselves a dump truck."

Rich's response was, "Yahoo!"

I picked my brother up, and we drove over to the landscaping company that had the truck for sale. We gave the landscaper the checks, and I drove the dump truck back to our landscape holding yard, our mulch storage bin, our employee parking lot, our dump, our EPA hazardous waste site, oh yeah, by the way, did I tell you my parents lived here? And then I went on back to Stuart Hall on the campus of the University of Dayton. I went to the snack bar and got another cheeseburger and went on up to my room. I opened up the door and again saw the light flashing on my message machine. I thought, "Cool. Somebody wants to celebrate, and gosh knows I'm sure in the mood to celebrate after getting my dump truck." It was my mom, and she had left me the following message: "Marty, I know you think you're real funny, but you can come right on back to this place that we have to call home that you've made such a mess, and you can take that dump truck back where you got it. We don't think it's funny. We told you you're not getting a dump truck, and you're not!"

131

Well, I called my mom back, she wasn't home, so I left her the following message. I said, "Mom, this is your wonderful son, Marty. But there's a little problem with the dump truck. I've lost the receipt, and Wal-Mart won't take it back."

But seriously, folks, I really felt like I knew what I was doing. And my confidence in my idea drove me. Things gradually started to improve for me in school as well. My grades got a little better. That year my company's sales hit $105,000 and I was financially free. By that, I mean I had paid for the dump truck, and I was paying for my college education at UD. The following year, things really started to blossom at Grunder Landscaping. My cousin, Dave Rado, who is a partner in the company today, joined the team in 1988. He made a wonderful difference. Dave Rado was the first of what have been many key additions to our company. Having great people has enabled me to grow Grunder Landscaping. In this case he enabled me to continue to pursue my degree and to get done. While I went to class, he saw to it that we installed and maintained the landscape jobs I had sold.

reality check

College will only teach you so much about managing people. You'll need to read books on leadership and leaders. And if going to college is not an option, enroll in a Dale Carnegie course (www.dalecarnegie.com) or go to one of the American Management Association's (www.amanet.org) many excellent seminars on management. Knowledge is confidence, and learning how to lead is an essential skill for running a business.

It gave Dave a great opportunity to show some of the talents he had for the landscape industry as well.

In 1989, Grunder Landscaping's sales were $259,000, and my grades got even better. The following year, 1990, with tears rolling down my face, and tears rolling down my mom's face, I graduated from the University of Dayton with a degree in business management! Sales for the company that year surpassed $300,000, and we were well on our way to success.

If you had asked me in 1986, after I was placed on academic probation, if I would make it through college, I would have told you, "No, I don't think so." But I mustered up enough courage and some confidence in myself, realized that I could do it, and went forward in that fashion.

Be Confident, but Listen!

If you need more inspiration, look at all the successful people you know who have overcome obstacles to become successful. You will be able to think of many, as most successful entrepreneurs struggle at some point, especially early on. They will give you some confidence to believe that you can do whatever your endeavor is. Here are a few things to ponder:

"IN ORDER TO SUCCEED,
YOU MUST KNOW WHAT YOU ARE DOING,
LIKE WHAT YOU ARE DOING,
AND BELIEVE IN WHAT YOU ARE DOING."

—Will Rogers

In 1944, NASA said that we would put a man on the moon in two hundred years, but we did it in twenty-five. In 1919, a team of engineers at Delco (or Dayton Engineering Laboratories) told the CEO and chief inventor, Charles Kettering, that they could paint a car in no less than thirty days. This was an improvement from the thirty-seven days it currently took. Thirty days to paint an automobile? Kettering wouldn't tolerate that. Kettering got it down to an hour by the end of 1919.

There is a difference between confidence and arrogance, however. Knowing your stuff is one thing, being a know-it-all is another. Successful people are confident, but they also know when to be quiet. How do you like being around someone who thinks he knows everything? It is no fun, and there really is little to learn from this type of person, so please don't be one.

You need to be confident and listen at the same time. Take an interest in people and what they do, and you'll learn a lot more than if you talk about yourself the whole time. Being cocky will turn so many people away that you'll have to move to another town to try again. Be focused on your goal and believe in yourself to the point you won't let failure bring you down. But don't be so focused that you lose sight of being able to learn from someone else. And please, try to be a person people want to be around.

Build Confidence in Those Who Help You, Too

For starters here, I don't like the word employee; I like "team member." Team member is a nice title for three reasons. For one, it is friendly and positive. Second, it's much more democratic—it doesn't imply that those who work for you are "lower" than you are. Thirdly, it really fits, because to be a successful entrepreneur, you must learn how to get a group or team all working together toward a common goal. The word, "employee" is a put-down and a self-centered word that I feel sets the stage for what you don't want—individuals pursuing their own agendas and ignoring the good of the whole company in the process.

You should see the nice look on new hires' faces at Grunder Landscaping Company when we tell them we don't have employees, only "team members." I also forbid my team members to call me their boss or ever say "I work for Marty." They are to say "I work with Marty and the great team at Grunder Landscaping Company." Sure, it's a little thing, but it makes a big difference.

I have tried, and you should try, to find out what makes people tick. When you learn how to get people to do what you want and need them to do and still have them love you, you can accomplish awesome things. I could sense this management skill was needed to be successful and knew I wanted to learn how to lead. Which is why I decided to pursue a degree in business management at the University of Dayton, rather than a degree in horticulture. To me, landscaping (and horticulture) was more like a hobby. I loved it! It was a passion that I gladly investigated on my own. And it would be much easier to learn on my own than business would be.

Confidence Will Keep Failures from Shutting You Down

It took Thomas Edison over eight hundred attempts before he got his light bulb to work. Orville and Wilbur Wright tested gliders for years before they were able to get off the ground and maintain a flight for any time and distance. Without those failures they never would have succeeded. Failure isn't a bad thing if viewed properly. As my friend Dick Lundy says, "I didn't fail, I just figured out the ways it wouldn't work." Without confidence failure will shut you down, and your goal will be unattainable. As my colleague on the speaking circuit Brian Tracy says, "If someone else has done what you want to do, that's all the proof in the world you need to believe you can do it too!" Think about that every time doubt creeps into your head.

You achieve self-confidence by learning how to do something well. Practice makes perfect. You achieve self-confidence by being around people who believe in you. Even Mr. Motivator Marty Grunder seeks out people who believe in me. This book is an excellent example of this. Writing a book is very difficult thing to do. It is frustrating, laborious, and draining. If it weren't for the positive feedback and constant encouragement and coaxing from many people, you would not have read one-third of what's in this book. Many folks believed in me, and I will write other books because of the confidence I now have in my writing abilities.

You may have to look hard, but eventually you'll find someone who believes in you. Some great sources of this kind of encouragement are: teachers, professors, priests, ministers, and especially other successful entrepreneurs. Those last folks understand better than anyone what one goes through to make a business work.

Now continue reading this book for more advice and inspiration!

chapter seven

Focus—
Get Rich in a Niche!

M any entrepreneurs have great difficulty focusing on their goals. It's a common problem. What is the most important thing I need to do today? This month? This year? Exactly what should I be doing? Many entrepreneurs even fall in love with the wrong focus. They fall in love with the clients or the marketplace when they should be falling in love with how they can specifically impact their clients' lives or solve a problem. They plow snow when they should be going to a boot camp or educational seminar. They focus on gross sales when they should focus on net profits. They may even lose sight of what business they're in. It is so easy to fall in love with a business idea and then watch it fall apart. Finding the right focus will prevent this.

Starting out Simple Is Smart

Many times entrepreneurs start out in a very basic business or at the low end of a particular industry. For example, when we started Grunder Landscaping Company in 1983, all my brother Rich and I did was cut grass, and we didn't even know how to do that very well. Gradually, from being in the industry, we learned how to do better.

Then we started to pay attention to and become interested in much more than grass cutting. We repeatedly were asked to prune shrubs, mulch beds, plant flowers, and seed and sod yards. Being energetic and enterprising, we tried pruning, mulching, planting, seeding, and sodding. When I reflect back on the quality of our first sod and seed jobs, I can only laugh. Our pruning was terrible as Rich and I became very good at turning shrubs into giant gumballs. Yuck! My team would really let me have it today if they found out how I used to do some of these things. Oh, and the thing we do best today—creative landscaping—was something we had no clue about back then. But you must start somewhere. And it is normal and quite smart to start out simple.

I've seen countless businesses try to do too much. They try to be everything to everybody, a sure way to dilute your service, affect profitability, and impede your endeavor.

Through the years businesses big and small have succumbed or stayed trapped in mediocrity as a result of a lack of focus. There are two schools of thought in business. One is that you should never put all your eggs in one basket. The logic of this theory is that you need to diversify and have multiple streams of income and thus lessen your risk of an overall failure. An example would be a restaurant that is doing reasonably well and starts a catering operation. This goes fairly well so they begin to sell lunches at a couple of office buildings around noon and take over the restaurant at a golf course. The entrepreneur thinks he is insulating himself from a downturn, or he thinks that since the original endeavor, one restaurant, was successful, the others will automatically be profitable too. Sometimes this is the case, but more times than not this lack of a focus will paralyze a firm. You have a choice—you can be fairly good at several things or the best at one thing. The latter is what we call "focus," and it is what you should do.

The most successful entrepreneurs focus on one thing and become the best in that category. By focusing on fewer things, all energies, strategies, and enthusiasm go into one endeavor. The restaurant owner who succeeds with the restaurant should look for ways to do what he or she does better. When it is felt that efficiency, production, and demand have all reached their peak, look to start the same operation in other marketplaces. The restaurant should look for other cities to operate in. If they have excelled at organization, operations, and systems, it can be done. McDonald's is a prime example.

Ray Kroc stumbled upon this wonderful little restaurant while selling them shake machines in 1954. He bought the restaurant from Dick and Mac McDonald. Forty-plus years later McDonald's serves as a case study in focus. Pepsi on the other hand was not focused and at one time owned Taco Bell, Pizza Hut, and Kentucky Fried Chicken. (Can you imagine being a Pepsi salesman trying to sell Pepsi to McDonald's? Why would McDonald's want to help a company that owns three of its competitors? McDonald's stayed with Coke.) For fun, check out Pepsi's ten-year performance on the stock exchange versus Coke and McDonald's. You will realize right away how powerful a focus is.

Finally in 1998, PepsiCo Inc. seemingly realized the error in a lack of focus and spun off their Taco Bell, Pizza Hut, and Kentucky Fried Chicken stores and formed a new company, Tricon Global Restaurants. With this focus, Tricon has improved and the restaurant business's future looks good for them. Chief Executive Officer of Tricon, David Novak, addressed the benefits of their new focus by saying, "Being part of PepsiCo, we didn't have the restaurant business in our bones. We never had a consistent approach, so we never got good at the basics.

It may be hard for you to believe a big company like PepsiCo had trouble with the basics, but the basics—the little things in business—are usually the reason a business works!

Put Your Eggs in One Basket!

The strategy to pursue is one of a clear, dedicated focus. In other words, put all your eggs in one basket and guard it with your life. Dorothy Lane Market, the grocery of choice for my family, is another great example of the power of focus.

Dorothy Lane Market was started in 1948 by Calvin Mayne and Frank Sakada. The name comes from the street the original store was located on. Today, with three stores in Dayton, Dorothy Lane Market enjoys annual sales of around one hundred million! They're not your average grocery store. They do things differently. One of the store's paramount strategies is a focus on offering only the best. Their prices are higher, but their quality and service are without question among the best in the industry.

Dorothy Lane Market was named Company of the Year in 1993 by *Supermarket Business* magazine, and Outstanding Specialty Food Retailer by the National Association for the Specialist Food Trade in 2001. They stand out in a crowd by being everything to a select group of people.

For years Dorothy Lane Market ran newspaper ads with coupons just like all other grocery stores. They felt they had to do this to generate business. Then with the invention of the technology to do so and some astute observations by Norman Mayne, the founder's son, they began to track their sales. In 1995 Club Dorothy

Lane Market was presented. This "club" entitled you to special pricing and privileges such as discounted services from several other local businesses vying for the same great clients that Dorothy Lane Market had. Each time you go through the checkout, you present a club DLM card. This is a small card that has a barcode on it that e-mails their software to track what you bought and how much you spent. After monitoring these sales results closely, Dorothy Lane Market realized that many of the coupon users were not regular customers. The coupon cutters came in, bought the "on sale" items, and left. Mr. Mayne immediately stopped producing the sales flyers and coupons and started mailing coupons and special deals to his best customers only. This controversial and gutsy call would prove to be a stroke of genius.

This strategy improved the store's efficiency and profitability, and did wonders for customer loyalty as well.

With huge stores in the same town such as Krogers, Meijers, Cub Foods, Super Kmart, Wal-Mart, and Sam's Club all selling groceries, Dorothy Lane Market continues to thrive. This is proof that a focus works. Other companies, such as Mercedes-Benz, Gucci, Polo, Nordstrom's, Coach leatherware, Dom Perignon champagne, and Walt Disney World also prove that consumers will pay to have the best products and services.

Dorothy Lane Market has proven that you can't be everything to everyone. Being everything to everyone is rarely profitable. Nor is it really fair. It's like dancing with someone other than the date who brought you. That philosophy is not likely to change as Norman's son Calvin believes in it, too. "We are always looking for ways to strengthen our focus," he said. "For example, while most supermarkets are scaling back their meat departments and focusing on pre-packaged cuts of meat, we are doing the opposite. We have expanded our meat counter, hired more quality meat cutters, and continue to try and give our customers what they ask for."

Being everything to a select few is the right thing to do, and it's usually very profitable. Get this very valuable secret unveiled early in your endeavor, and you'll see a huge difference in the long run. A number of studies have proven that eighty percent of your business will come from twenty percent of your clients, but we don't usually set our endeavors up to focus eighty percent of our time on that twenty percent. Many entrepreneurs do the opposite—spend eighty percent (or more) of their time on the part that generates twenty percent of their business!

Dorothy Lane Market has a superb reputation and terrific brand awareness in Dayton, Ohio. You'll never see them diversifying into other endeavors like Dorothy Lane Market gas stations, Dorothy Lane Market dry cleaning, Dorothy Lane Market hardware superstore, or Dorothy Lane Market jewelry. They know one thing very well and that's running a fine grocery store catering to picky, knowledgeable clients who are willing to pay more to get more. And if you're a customer who spends enough, you'll even get a gourmet turkey at the holidays on the house. Not only does Dorothy Lane Market have all their eggs in one basket, but they have their wine, seafood, bakery, dairy, and gourmet foods in it too. And please don't try to take anything out of their basket, or you'll lose your hand; they are very tough to compete with on service—their focus. (See www.dorothylane.com.) They found this focus by listening to their clients.

Clay Mathile preaches "focus" to anyone who listens. And you should listen. Clay's old company, the Iams Corporation, had the technology, knowledge, and ability to do for horses' and other large animals' nutrition what they did for dogs and cats. But they never did. Some people are overly optimistic, and in their quest to make a buck, they don't see the challenges and problems associated with an endeavor that is outside your present experience. Clay was approached many times about applying Iams' knowledge to the equine industry. Each time Clay said no because he realized it would dilute his company's main focus and was contrary to Iams' mission "to improve the well-being of dogs and cats." It did not say horses so they did not pursue it.

This philosophy worked well and enabled Iams to become the best in dog and cat nutrition. Clay advised me to "Build a company that is an industry leader. Be the best." He then went on to simply, yet effectively, point out to me several problems with what I was doing with my two companies. He said, "You have to decide what you want to do and then create a world-class organization." Never once did he directly mention size. He talked about narrowing my focus. He showed me that even though I thought we were king of landscaping in Dayton, we weren't. We really only had about three to five percent of the market cornered. "Get forty or fifty percent and that's something to be proud of," he said. I owe Clay a lot. He is the reason for this chapter. He taught me the lesson of focus in an entrepreneurial endeavor. Grunder Landscaping Company doesn't have forty percent of the market yet, but at least we have a focus, and we've quit being everything to everyone. But this wasn't always the case. If you called us and asked us to clean out your garage, we said yes. If you called with a job that would be given to the lowest bidder, we came and begged to be the lowest bidder. If there were a client holding on line 2 and a prospect on line 1, we had the receptionist tell the client we'd call them back and take the call from the prospect. It went even further than that.

In 1989, while I was still in college, I purchased a $25,000 van with a high-powered pressure washer in it. I named the company "GrimeBusters," which proved to be the only smart thing I did with this endeavor. I thought I could make a bunch of money washing patios, decks, and fleets of trucks. I was overconfident since my landscaping company was doing so well. My poor planning and forgetting to think about basic goals cost me dearly. Eighteen months and $15,000 later, without the business to support the monthly payment for the equipment and with no time to focus on this endeavor, I sold GrimeBusters for one dollar.

But the lesson I learned was worth much more than that. The lesson was: don't forget what got you where you are today. And just because one endeavor works well doesn't mean others will. Unfortunately, I still didn't totally get this focus thing and made a few more mistakes. This time, the mistakes were less severe.

Learn To Say No

Most entrepreneurs live off the thrill of starting things. We are for the most part very confident people who almost feel unbeatable. We are very creative and are looking constantly for new, exciting ventures. We only think of the dollars being deposited, not the dollars being withdrawn to run these endeavors. And this was my outlook. I tried to offer gift baskets to my clients one winter, which was a disaster. Why? No one bought them, and it is no wonder. What would a landscaper know about fancy fruit and gift baskets? The answer? Little. I sold Christmas trees for three years, too, which was plenty of fun but not profitable. Not only was it not profitable, but it prohibited us from doing landscaping work. In fact, we turned away landscaping which

reality check

Success in business is as much about what you don't do as what you choose to do. If you don't think you should be doing something or taking on a job, trust your instinct. Business is about having fun and making money. By saying no, you can often be happier and make more money. Learn how to say no nicely, and it will reward you greatly if you have the guts to do it.

was what we do and which was profitable to sell Christmas trees which was not profitable. We also for the longest time installed sod, mowed lawns, raked leaves, and just about anything else clients or prospects asked us to do. This is common for entrepreneurs; they often don't know how to say no. Today, we are very careful about what work we take on. If it is something not offered on our "menu," we won't do it. If the request is not part of our focus, we say no thank you. Here's exactly what we say, "I'm sorry, Grunder Landscaping Company doesn't do that because it would prohibit us from being the best designers, installers, and caretakers of creative landscaping in Dayton. Here's a list of what we do offer; I hope we can help you with one of these offerings sometime."

As each year goes by, it only proves more powerfully how profitable a focus can be. Our focus at Grunder Landscaping Company is the creative design, installation, and maintenance of landscaping. We arrived at this focus by performing a SWOT analysis of our company in which our whole team played a role. A SWOT (SWOT stands for Strengths, Weaknesses, Opportunities, and Threats) analysis is

reality check

You should be constantly fine tuning your business and focusing on what you do best. Part of this process involves abandoning business as you grow. You should abandon any business that: (1) Is not profitable. (2) Is work that potentially damages your reputation. For example, if you are known for high-end quality remodeling work, you should strongly consider abandoning any work that does not fit that description. Imagine what would happen to Rolex watches' reputation if you could buy them at Kmart. (3) You also don't want undertakings that take too many resources to perform for the profits generated. In other words, ask yourself what better things you could be doing with the resources being allocated toward low-profit work. (4) Abandon, too, any services or products that you can't be a market leader in. If you can't be the best, don't do it.

a self-analysis of yourself, your staff, and your company. And it is a very effective exercise for examining the current state of your endeavor and pointing out some solutions and opportunities that will help you become more successful. We realized what we were best at. We uncovered our competitive advantage. Had I learned this lesson eight years earlier, I'd have much more money than I do now.

This is what happens when you have too many endeavors. Rarely does it work well.

Many entrepreneurs try to be all things to all people and that usually doesn't work. Pretty soon, you've become too diluted. Know your niche and stay in it. Know it very, very well, and you'll get rich in that niche.

Another Kind of Focus You Can't Forget

We've talked about focusing on the type of business that makes the most sense for you, but there's another kind of focus you can't forget. You also need to focus, as you go through each day and week, on the critical issues that dramatically affect your business. In many cases this means you will have to do things that you don't enjoy doing. But successful entrepreneurs know how to identify what needs to be done and focus on those things. I call these types of issues Critical Success Factors or CSFs. These are things that *must* be done to become successful. These CSFs need to be put in writing; that way they become real.

In 1990, right after I graduated from the University of Dayton with a degree in business management, I knew I had a lot of work to do. Still in somewhat the academic mode, I often would go to the library at UD to work on my business plan and goals. During these quiet hours I was able to think about where I wanted to go. I still have the piece of paper I carried in my wallet for years that had my critical success factors on it. There were just three at that time:

1. Sell landscaping

2. Keep expenses low

3. Bill and collect promptly

Thanks to the help and encouragement of my many college professors and mentors, I stayed focused on those three CSFs for a good four years. In fact, those three CSFs are still on my list today along with many more short- and long-term CSFs. Basically, for four years if the task didn't involve selling landscaping, keeping expenses low, or billing/collecting, I rarely did it. This was a very hard thing to do. And if it weren't for my partner, Dave Rado, I never could have done it. He installed landscapes and took care of production.

Many times I wanted to do something else. Sometimes it was something fun that tried to distract me, like going out of town on a golf outing with my friends. Other times it was talking on the phone with a friend when I should have been getting bills out. Still other times it was avoiding my main vice on a Saturday of going to the racetrack to watch the horses (I didn't and still don't bet much on horses) instead of going out to sell landscapes. I even gave up another interest of mine—wanting to be a thoroughbred race announcer—because I couldn't spend the time it would have taken to become great at it. My main goal was to become a successful entrepreneur, and some distractions, even though I enjoyed them, had to be put aside.

This lack of a CSF focus keeps many aspiring entrepreneurs from being successful.

Up to this point, we've talked about six steps to success. We've talked about picking a passion. You were instructed to set goals. We've discussed getting paid to learn. We've talked about surrounding yourself with winners. And in the last chapter we spoke of believing in yourself.

Now I have shown you the power of a focus, but we're not done yet. I hope you're as excited about entrepreneurship as I am about helping you. Great! Read on. Don't stop here.

chapter eight

Ask Questions

"When I am faced with a decision . . .
I dredge up every scrap of knowledge I can.
I call in people, I phone them, I read
whatever I can get my hands on. I use my intellect
to inform my instincts to test all this data.
'Hey, instinct, does this sound right,
does it smell right, does it feel right?'"

—Colin Powell, Secretary of State

Whether you're twelve, thirty, or eighty, you surely remember at some point in your life sitting in a class or an environment like a class and being afraid to raise your hand and ask a question for fear that your question was silly, people would laugh, and you'd be embarrassed. Or that really you ought to know that answer, and there's no reason for you to ask a question like that! No one else has that question, so why should I? Folks, people have retired wealthy writing books titled "Everything You Always Wanted to Know about X, but Were Afraid to Ask," putting on seminars teaching people simple concepts, and paying people like myself to improve other people's self-confidence. I myself, for a long time, was afraid to ask questions. I lacked self-confidence. I was afraid someone would make fun of me if I had a question. I thought others might think I was dense, or ignorant. But, until I got the answers to all these questions I had, I couldn't gain the knowledge I needed to get the confidence I lacked. As my late Uncle Ron would always say, "Knowledge is confidence," and this is probably one of the truest statements you'll ever come across. Plain and simple, once you learn how to do something or learn about something, your fears will go away because you know how to do it. Pilots are not afraid to fly because they know their job and understand flying and airplanes. Through classes, flight simulators, and training, pilots are well prepared. Many questions have been asked, and answered, and much guesswork eliminated. Doctors aren't afraid to operate because they have been trained and conditioned to react to many scenarios that could occur during an operation.

Gradually, the knowledge I was gaining from the University of Dayton, combined with all my interest in business and success, boosted my confidence. I was well on my way. I really felt that I could do what I wanted to do—that I could turn Grunder Landscaping Company into a multimillion dollar operation someday. But many questions had to be asked.

Some of you reading this book right now may be either high school or college students, and if you are a student, I strongly recommend that you learn to question everything. Even ask the questions that seem hard to ask. Case in point, every year I mentor a young man or woman at the University of Dayton. We're instructed by the University to answer any questions they might have, to help guide them on to a proper choice of jobs and, basically, to just be there as a sounding board. It's a wonderful program and students, professors, and mentors all enjoy it and benefit from it. I know I've learned a ton from it. While meeting with a student once, I could tell the young man had a question but he was very hesitant about it. I finally said, "Scott, you seem like you're afraid to ask me something. What's bothering you?"

"Oh, nothing," he said.

And I said, "All right, I know you want to ask me a question, but for whatever reason, you're afraid to do so, and we're going to sit here and keep drinking milkshakes until you tell me what your question is."

Finally, he broke down. Bear in mind, this is a junior, a young man in the third year of the business school of the University of Dayton, and he said to me, "Marty, I've been taking classes toward a degree in marketing for almost three years now. I still don't know what a marketing major does once his gets his diploma. Could you please tell me?"

> "MILLIONS SAW THE APPLE FALL
> BUT NEWTON WAS
> THE ONE TO ASK WHY."
>
> —Bernard Baruch, businessman, statesman

Now, many of you, at this point, might be laughing. But I really didn't think it was too funny. This poor fellow had picked marketing as a major while he was a senior in high school, and he really had no idea what it was about. "That's a very good question," I said, and then went on to discuss what marketing majors might do. I told him, "You might get a job at the Marriott Corporation working in the advertising department, you might get a job at Xerox selling copiers,

151

you might get a job working for a small business helping them position their brand appropriately." The point here is that it's impossible to sit in a classroom and try to figure out what exactly you're going to do once you get that diploma. I don't blame this young man for this. Universities need to do a better job of teaching more about the "real world." On the other hand, they can't do everything so **you** must learn to ask questions.

When you don't get answers to your questions, you only prolong the time it takes to achieve your goals and be successful. There's a very good chance that the answer to one of those questions might be all you need to unlock the secret to your future or to your success.

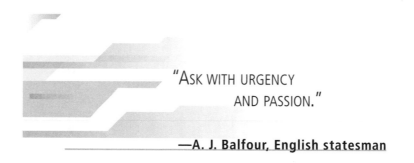

"ASK WITH URGENCY
AND PASSION."

—A. J. Balfour, English statesman

Write Those Questions Down!

I work with a lot of entrepreneurs—businessmen and women all over the United States and Canada, and as I mentioned earlier I suggest they all carry what is called a "pocket briefcase." These are available from the Levenger Corporation. Visit them online at www.levenger.com. A pocket briefcase is full of 3" x 5" note cards, and it fits neatly in your back pocket or purse. I never go anywhere without my little pocket briefcase. In it, I have cards on which I've written down what my long-term goals are, what my immediate goals are, my to-do list, and any questions that may come to me while I'm sitting on an airplane, waiting for an appointment, or maybe even sitting in church, or at a basketball game. When a thought comes to my mind, I write it down immediately. To achieve a goal, you have to be very focused. Once you lose focus on that goal, forget it. Since I always have my life in my back pocket, I can write things down whenever I need to—a new goal I'd like to put on my master list, a new item for my to-do list, or perhaps most important of all, a question I've thought of that I need to get an answer for. How many times have you said to someone, "Oh, I wanted to ask you something I was thinking about the other day, but I forgot what it was"? If you're always carrying something to record notes on or in, and a pen, then you'll always be able to write down your ideas or your questions. This is very, very important.

As one of my best friends Dick Lundy, says,

"There is no magical book you can find help for everything in.

So a problem is only as large as your inability to solve it."

Dick ought to know. He trains thoroughbred racehorses. Horses can't talk, and they can be a big puzzle at times because of it. Next to my late father, Dick is the most patient and inquisitive man I know. I've seen Dick work with a horse for over a year before it runs. I've seen Dick train a horse for a year only to have it get hurt, come back, train for another six months, get hurt again and come back, and then finally run in a race. Each time he would question himself and the horse. "Am I using the right equipment? Does this animal ache someplace I am missing? Does this equine athlete not get firm footing on the race track? Would he or she run better on grass?" His patience has paid off. In 1991 he won the prestigious

$1,000,000 Breeder's Cup Turf race with a long shot named Opening Verse that no one other than Dick Lundy thought would win. Dick knows to be successful with horses you have to be patient . . . and ask questions.

I grew up in a rural area where most people did a lot of things themselves. Our neighbors and my family made their own repairs, built things, and tackled many projects that the average everyday person would not. It was a way of life for our family. My dad fixed everything. The cars, the washer, the dryer, our toys, the tractors, and he even fixed the furnace. He tackled projects like installing central air conditioning, adding on to the house, heck; he even built our house, and poured concrete everywhere. I am still, to this day, amazed at the things my dad knew. My little secret of success "Ask questions" comes from my father. Anytime he needed to do something, he would go to the expert in that area and ask questions about how it was done. He also listened very carefully, talking very little. He repeated this exercise so many times over the eighteen or so years I was around him at home, I couldn't help but learn from his humble approach to learning how to do something—by getting answers to his questions. Most people don't operate like this, though. Especially men. It's a pride thing. An ego thing.

Paul Allen, whom I introduced to you earlier, asked Ed Roberts question after question. Those answers helped him launch Microsoft. Today, Allen's estimated net worth is 28 billion dollars. And in many ways Ed Roberts' answers to Allen's questions in 1974 *made* Microsoft.

You should also question why everyday things happen. Let me explain. These are things that happen every day that can inspire an idea for your business or for a whole new business.

In 1948, Swiss engineer George de Mestral was about to go to dinner with his wife when she had trouble with the zipper on her dress. She told George there had to be a better way to secure fabrics. George logged that thought away. Shortly after that de Mestral returned from a walk in the woods with his dog. As he was brushing the burrs off that had accumulated on the dog's coat, he asked himself, "I wonder how that works?" He quickly examined the burrs under a microscope and saw that each burr had a surface with tiny hooks. These hooks stuck to his clothes very well. Due to de Mestral's asking questions, he developed Velcro which earned him millions in royalties.

Asking Questions Saves Time and Money

Once a person can admit to himself that he doesn't know everything, then he can make the leap to admitting this to others by asking questions. Try it. Once you start asking questions, you will shorten the time it takes to be successful at your endeavor. Think about it. Why go out and beat your head against the wall trying to figure out how to go about something that you don't know how to do? Go seek out the right people and ask questions. Imagine the last time you had computer trouble, for instance, and tried to work through it yourself. What happened? There's a very good chance that, after several hours of trying, you gave up and had to call someone anyway or, worse yet, maybe you damaged the computer even further, all because you didn't want to ask for help. Now, how smart is that? It's a waste of time and money not to ask questions. Successful people watch their time closely. Money can be replaced—time cannot—making it, in my mind, the most valuable thing in the world! Even the world's wealthiest person can't buy time!

I'm lazy to a degree, I admit it. I refuse to do something I know nothing about, or to flounder around trying to do something when I have no idea of how. I'm also a skeptical person who always asks questions. I don't automatically believe everything I read or come across, and I constantly seek reaffirmation of a particular conclusion or belief. I realized a long time ago that asking questions is a very healthy and beneficial exercise. There is no way I would have the successful business I have if it weren't for all the questions I've asked.

Once I started my business, I was anxious to learn. I interrogated all of the other professional landscapers on our lunch breaks at the fast food joints. I also spent countless hours at garden centers, nurseries, and seminars learning techniques, observing workers, reading plant tags, and asking questions. Some of the questions I asked of other landscapers were: How do professionals edge a bed? How do professionals plant trees? How do you mow a lawn and make it look like the lawn at Candlestick Park I dreamt of? Are there better ways to control weeds than pulling them?

I also spent several days riding in a lawn care truck with Mark Grunkemeyer right after he started Buckeye Ecocare. Mark taught me a lot about how to care for turf. Today, Mark's company is a multimillion-dollar success, but he took the time to answer my questions when he was a small two-man operation.

But there were many other questions I needed to ask that had nothing to do with landscaping. Running a business is not easy. You have to know how to perform the service you're offering and/or construct or manufacture the product you're offering. You have to know the ins and outs of many business practices as well. Today at Grunder Landscaping Company, I am to the stage of my business that I can spend much of my time staying on top of the most up-to-date, best practices in business. My associates stay up on the latest developments and best practices in landscaping and horticulture. I still read a lot on horticultural and landscaping design. But I have others constantly briefing and teaching me and my teammates about horticulture, so I no longer have to have that as my main focus. My main focus now is business and as a CEO that is where it should be.

Some Questions To Ask Fellow Entrepreneurs

I am constantly meeting with others asking them questions about how they run their business. Here's some questions I regularly ask fellow entrepreneurs:

1. **How's business?** It's good to get a feel from others on this as an informal gauge of the economy. Many times you may be alerted to a trend that could help you capitalize on an opportunity, or conversely, avoid a problem. For example, if enough people say their backlog of work is very strong, maybe you would go ahead with a marketing campaign. By asking this question, you can learn a lot.

2. **How do you attract new clients?** The product or service from business to business may be different, but marketing can be very similar. I've gotten many great ideas from other entrepreneurs as to how they attract new clients. On one occasion, I found a fellow entrepreneur had the same high net worth clients that we were targeting. He shared his mailing list with us, and we mailed our newsletter to his clients. We quickly gained several new clients as a result.

157

All this from asking a question. Many times asking questions stimulates ideas and new business.

3. **What major obstacles have you had in becoming successful?** This is a great question. Finding out what problems others have overcome is very helpful and could save you time and money. I asked this question of a successful entrepreneur in 1989. He advised me to have at least two banks that knew and understood my business. At the time, I only had one banking relationship. I went out that next week and met another banker. Three months later that proved very valuable as I needed $10,000 to buy another truck, and my bank wouldn't loan it to me. The other bank gladly did loan me the money. Had I not asked that question, I never would have known how important a diversified banking relationship is.

4. **If you had it to do all over again, what would you do?** What would you *not* do? Again, why not avoid mistakes?

5. **Can I tour your operation?** This is one of my favorite things to do. Not only do owners like sharing their own facilities, but you will also learn a lot of neat ideas.

reality check

Just asking the questions is only half the job of this step. The other half is listening carefully, recording the answers on paper, and taking action on them.

6. What consultants have you used? Who was good? There are a lot of good consultants who can really help you. But there are a lot of bad ones, too, and a phone call or meeting would help you avoid a problem.

When my brother and I started Grunder Landscaping Company, our young age, desire to learn, politeness, and obvious lack of experience motivated people to help us. Contrary to the pessimists' belief, most of the people you will ever meet are kind, good-hearted folks who want to help. Teaching is one of the most rewarding things to do. Think of a time you shared your knowledge with someone. How did that feel? It feels good to help someone learn how to do something. I'll never get tired of teaching.

Through the years my ability to ask questions has shortened the time it normally takes to become successful. In fact, over seventy-five percent of the businesspeople and entrepreneurs who consult me are much older than me! By age twenty-five I had a million-dollar-a-year business in an industry where only ten percent of all companies have sales of one million of greater. I don't think I am smarter than anyone else; I think I may have read more, sought out more successful people, and asked more questions than anyone else in my industry.

Let People Know You Want to Know!

Becoming known as someone who seeks out—and takes—advice is a good thing. The people I work with at my companies, my family, friends, and clients all know I want feedback. Once the people around you and involved with your endeavor know you accept feedback, it will come!

You can create this healthy, learning environment several ways. For starters, if you just ask questions frequently, people get a hint of your desire to learn and be the best you can be. Because of all the questions I asked, people such as my high school teachers, college professors, family, and other entrepreneurs would do other things to help me learn. Because of my enthusiasm and obvious desire to be successful, people helped me by giving me books to read, suggesting other classes to take, referring mentors to me, and even giving me jobs to do at their homes, which was very important early on in my success.

The thing to remember here is that people can't help you if they don't know you need help. When you start asking questions, people will do some amazing things for you.

You will also do some amazing things for yourself once the questions are answered.

chapter nine

Perform in a Way That's Contrary to the Norm

*"Different isn't always better,
but better is always different."*

—Dale Dauten

Perform in a way that's contrary to the norm is my fancy way of saying, "Be different."

To be successful in business, I firmly believe that you must be different. For your entrepreneurial endeavor to succeed, you're going to have to find out a way to do what you're doing a little bit differently than the way everyone else is doing it.

My friend Dan Kennedy, in Phoenix, Arizona, is a very successful speaker, author, and consultant (see www.dankennedy.com). He wrote a very good book called *How to Succeed in Business by Breaking All the Rules*. The whole book is dedicated to doing things differently, and I think that's the way you have to look at your business or your entrepreneurial endeavor to succeed.

A guy named Fred Smith figured this out. You probably see his white trucks with purple and orange writing on them rushing through your city each and every day. His company is a multibillion-dollar one with a worldwide presence, and its motto used to be

"Absolutely, positively overnight." It's since been changed to "The World on Time." By now you probably know I'm talking about the corporation Federal Express, or FedEx, as it's called now. FedEx has become so successful that their company's name has entered the language. Ever notice how we call something a "Kleenex" rather than a tissue, say we need a "Xerox" rather than a copy, or when we need a drink, call it a "Coke" whether it is one or not? These famous brand names either originated the product in question or are so popular they are inseparable from it in the public's mind. The same is true of FedEx. We say we need to FedEx something, whether we're using FedEx or not. But you might be shocked to know that Fred Smith, the founder of FedEx, received a "C" for his idea while he was in college. That's right, a "C." The professor said it just wouldn't work. Fred Smith disagreed and he built FedEx by being different and basically re-engineering the speed business is conducted at. He thought people would pay well for convenience, and he was right, but thirty years ago this was a very different idea.

The second company I'd like to talk to you about is a 15 billion-dollars-a-year corporation based in Minnesota. In 1977, they invented a little yellow piece of paper with a gummy strip on one side that enabled you to write on that paper and stick it anywhere—on the TV, on the dashboard, or on top of another note that you were passing around at work. This corporation is called the 3M Corporation, and the stick note they invented now accounts for more than a billion dollars a year of their annual sales! Just because they did something a little bit differently than everyone else. The stick note is something so simple it was right beneath our eyes all the while, but we chose not to pursue it. You have to think in a way that is contrary to the norm because that little secret will help get you noticed, and get you where you want to be.

David Gold knows how to be different. In 1982 he founded 99 Cents Only Stores. Today, they have over a hundred stores in southern California and Nevada and sales of over $360 million a year. This wonderful success story too has its roots in being different. As a young boy Gold remembered being refused service in a department store at 8:55 p.m. because the store closed at 9:00. You've surely experienced this retail practice. You know the dirty looks you get when you walk into a store five to ten minutes before closing. Well, Gold didn't like that, either. Consequently, all 99 Cents Only Stores are open from 9 a.m. to 9 p.m. But managers know to open the doors before 9:00 a.m. and close after 9:00 p.m. and they never pressure customers into checking out; after all, buying customers are why 99 Cents Only is successful.

All 99 Cents Only Stores have plenty of bright lights, are very clean and airy, and their shelves are fully stocked. Why? Because many discount stores are dark, dingy, and cluttered. Many big retailers play games (talk to anyone who does business with them) when it comes to paying their bills, not 99 Cents Only. They have never been late with a payment, and vendors love doing business with them because they are known for "treating people the way they'd want to be treated."

Even in their advertising 99 Cents Only stands out in the crowd. At each store opening, nine 19" color TV's are sold for 99¢. Once those are gone nine microwaves are sold for 99¢. Needless to say, long lines form outside the stores days before their grand opening. Those long lines attract the media and create a tremendous amount of excitement for a store selling goods for 99¢ each. Everything that Gold does in his stores centers around being different, but it is only different because few other retailers use Gold's uncanny common sense. His ability to look for simple things like opening and closing the stores earlier and later than the posted hours and selling televisions for 99¢ makes his venture successful. As you're working on your entrepreneurial venture, think of ways you can be different. If you look hard enough, the answer is probably right under your nose.

The Krispy Kreme Edge

Doughnuts are doughnuts, right? Sure they are. No, not really. There's one company that today is wildly profitable and successful selling something that you or I could easily make in our own kitchen. I'm talking about the Krispy Kreme Doughnut Corporation based in Winston-Salem, North Carolina. This company has customers so loyal that these doughnuts are now legendary. In 1999, when a Krispy Kreme store opened in Los Angeles, people drove for more than fifty miles away to stand in line. If you don't have a Krispy Kreme doughnut shop in your town right now, within the next five years you probably will. I believe they are another Starbuck's in the making. I know doughnuts.

Krispy Kreme doughnuts *are* delicious, and the company and stores are extremely well run. But the real reason for their success is the fact that they do things a little bit differently than everyone else.

You may be salivating, and you would probably like to go get a Krispy Kreme doughnut right now. Let me paint you a picture of their store. When you walk in, you'll see behind a pristine glass window a conveyor belt carrying doughnuts through a doughnut assembly line. This process is amazing. A parade of doughnuts is mixed and cut, and then floats right on down through the fryer, flipping over automatically halfway through the cooking process.

The doughnuts then jump onto a conveyor that whisks them out of the shortening and into a glistening cascade of glaze. Clean, uniformed employees with little sticks gather up the fresh, warm doughnuts and usually place them in boxes as there are people waiting for them. Nothing is hidden. You will never wonder what might have happened to your doughnuts; you can see it all! The store is a place that you need to visit because therein lies their secret.

It's not really the doughnuts, although the doughnuts are delicious. It's the aura, the production, and the show that Krispy Kreme puts on every day. They were wise enough not to hide the production of the doughnuts. You can see that everything is clean. You can see the doughnuts coming on down. Krispy Kreme is a place you want to take your kids to. Krispy Kreme is somewhat magical. This production in each store is only the finale of a carefully choreographed process that is completely controlled from the brick buildings on Ivy Avenue in Winston-Salem, North Carolina. Consider these statistics on Krispy Kreme doughnuts: every day there are more than 3.5 million Krispy Kreme doughnuts sold; there are 12,000 dozen sold every hour.

The next time you see a Krispy Kreme doughnut shop, go in and compare what they do to any other doughnut shop. Dunkin' Donuts, for example, is a boring doughnut shop. Nothing about their store is anything you'd talk about with others. A Krispy Kreme store is. Krispy Kreme is a perfect example of a company doing something very simple very, very well and very differently than anyone else.

Damon Bailey, the fabled basketball player from Heltonville, Indiana, owns several Krispy Kreme doughnut shops in Ohio and Michigan. To quote Damon: "Maybe I shouldn't be saying this, but it costs almost nothing to make doughnuts, and you can charge a lot to sell them. If you know what to do with the basics, you can end up with something everybody loves, something everybody thinks is kind of special."

Zig When Everyone Else Is Zagging

To succeed beyond the ordinary level in any business, you must be different. Go with the current trends, and you'll receive ordinary returns. Dare to be different, and you'll be rewarded with better than average returns. Sometimes you'll get a huge return for being different. I have a successful friend and client, Dave Tucker of Sensible Software in Ijamsville, Maryland, who says, "You need to zig when everyone else is zaggin'." Well put, Dave.

There's all kinds of things you can do to accomplish this. I know a real estate agency in New York that, after visiting a potential client, follows up with a nice brownie and a note that says "If you think the brownie's sweet, you should try our services at XYZ Real Estate Company." If you don't think that little things like this make a big difference, take a trip to England and look at the castles. Those castles have doors that are thirty and forty feet tall ... moved by little two-inch hinges. As W. Clement Stone observed, "Little hinges swing big doors." Have you ever been stepped on by an elephant? Probably not. Have you ever been stung by a mosquito? Most likely. Well you could go to Africa and not get killed by an elephant, but get stung by a mosquito and die of malaria. Yes, it's true. Little things make a big difference.

My first client was Marty Clark, and he knows the value of being different, too. Marty sells labels and signs to large corporations for packaging. He is a very successful salesperson, and I think

reality check

As you may have noticed reading this book, I refer to the people I do business with as clients, not customers. Client is defined as "a person who engages the professional advice or services of another." The word client implies a relationship is present. To succeed in business you need any advantage you can get. Our entire team at Grunder Landscaping feels we are the best, and, therefore, we have clients, not just customers. Small things like this can make a big difference.

his sense of humor contributes to his success. A while ago I had to call Marty at work. He wasn't in so I got his voice mail. This is what his message said: "Hi, this is Marty. I can't come to the phone right now as I'm out wild boar hunting in Africa. If you'd like to speak to a real person, dial xx and speak to Kathy. Otherwise, leave a message and I'll get back to you." In a world of stuffy corporate correctness, sometimes humor goes a long way. When appropriate, being funny gets you noticed and makes you easy to remember. This is also Bert Anderson's approach.

Something Fishy Here!

Bert Anderson was tired of being on the road as a corporate sales trainer. He'd learned several things from his job, though. Number one, he learned from eating out at hundreds of different restaurants that great food and service are the secrets of success in that business. Second, he learned that people make a difference—your business won't work without good people. Lastly, Bert learned that to be successful you must be different. And Bert *is* different.

In 1985 Bert started Theo Thudpucker's Raw Bar on North Hutchinson Island in Ft. Pierce, Florida. Theo is a fictional character created by Bert. After all, what sounds better, Bert Anderson's or Theo Thudpucker's? I started eating at Theo's in 1993 when my wife and I first visited there on our honeymoon. One step inside Theo's, and you quickly see something different.

For starters the place is very small but full of funny, entertaining pictures and trinkets. None are more fun than Theo himself. The restaurant is really an extension of his personality. (The menu is mostly seafood although they have about the best cheeseburger I've ever eaten.) Many times Theo (Bert) greets you with a big "Hello, welcome to Theo's." The first time we went in there he asked us if we'd like a seat by the window. We innocently said, "Yes, that would be great."

Theo (Bert) led us to our table. He seated us and immediately walked away. "Wait!" I said, "I thought we could have a seat by the window?"

Theo replied, "You're correct, just a second, sir!" We then observed Theo pushing a large plate glass window on wheels out to our table.

"There you are, folks! A seat by the window!"

I looked at my wife, and we both burst out laughing. I was hooked, wondering what was coming next.

Two minutes later Theo came back around and interrupted the waitress and asked us if we'd ever had smoked fish.

My wife gullibly said, "No, is that your specialty?"

"It sure is, would you like to see it?"

"Sure!" my wife exclaimed.

A minute later there came Theo with a fish on a stick with a lit cigarette in his mouth. This time I nearly fell out of my chair. For the next hour I watched Theo (Bert) go through his shtick to the other patrons. Everyone enjoyed him and the food. Theo Thudpucker's is not the only restaurant on the island, but it is the busiest. Bert Anderson has realized that being different is a big part of being successful. People go to Theo's for the great food, but they also go there because the place is different. Different in a good way.

Most restaurants seat you, feed you, take your money, and shove you out the door. Not at Theo's. At Theo's Bert Anderson will feed you, entertain you, make you feel great, bill you, thank you, and walk you to the door. Truly better is always different!

A Savvy Grandmother's Secrets

In horse racing, the difference between winning and losing can be less than an inch. In 1996, Grindstone won the Kentucky Derby by a nose over Cavenier. Literally, less than an inch. But, today, Grindstone is the horse that is remembered. Quickly—who did Bill Clinton defeat in 1992? Who was the runner-up in last year's NCAA men's basketball tournament? No one remembers who finished second. In life, the difference between winning and losing can also be the slimmest of margins. Not many people remember the losers, unless you're Susan Lucci. Often little adjustments or little things make all the difference. As is the case with Betty at the shoeshine stand at the Cincinnati-Northern Kentucky Airport.

I frequent this airport a lot and have gotten to know her well. She has shared this stand with many different people since 1992, but Betty is still there, and the previous co-workers still can't figure out why Betty makes great money and loves her job. As Betty says,

"I'm a people person. I love to talk." I've watched her and uncovered the secret of her success. She builds rapport with her clients and talks to them. All the other people who work next to her just shine shoes. They don't say anything. Through the years, Betty has learned how to start a conversation with travelers. I've heard her so many times, I've got her routine down pat.

The first question she asks is "Where are you headed?" Betty is a bright lady. She's learned that the fifteen minutes she takes every morning to study the weather across the nation enables her to strike common ground with her clients. It starts a friendship. So when they say where they're flying to, she tells them what kind of weather to expect. Striking common ground with your clients is a critical first step to success. Clients won't open their wallets to you until they trust you, until they think you are their friend. Trust is built over time, but it only takes Betty about five minutes to shine a pair of shoes. So she has to work very quickly to get a good tip and lobby for repeat business. Many of her clients love to see her just for the weather reports. It won't be long, and Betty will be selling weather reports.

If a customer has very dirty shoes (most of her customers are men), she'll ask her second question, "Did your kids win their ball game?" Most people are amazed that she even knew they had kids. She responds, "I could tell by the condition of your shoes that you've been out with kids on the ball diamond." Usually this question opens up a whole conversation about kids. Betty talks about her six grandchildren and how she and her husband love to take them places. Now what parent wouldn't tip such a nice grandma and want to come back and talk?

Betty never went to college. At least I don't think she did. I'm not even sure she finished high school. But she always asks her clients what business they're in. And from there she engages in more rapport-building behavior. Through the years Betty has learned a lot about business this way.

Not only does Betty know business, but she does very well at a series of little things that bond her with her clients. All very simple, yet very different, and contrary to the norm. Why? Because most shoeshine people don't act like this. They shine your shoes, they say "Thanks. Have a great day," and move on to the next one. Major corporations seemingly can't figure out what Betty has, or do what this little grandma in Cincinnati has done. Maybe the airport should make her vice president of marketing. By the way, one morning I came in on the redeye from Los Angeles at 5:30 in the morning. As I was getting in my truck in the parking lot, I saw Betty park her black, shiny new Lincoln Continental just next to mine. I asked her what the weather was going to be like that day. She said stormy and flights would be delayed. Bad day for travelers—good day for her as delays and bad weather mean people with time on their hands and dirty shoes. Judging by her car and my business intuition, I think she may be more successful than many of the people she shines shoes for!

The Hundred Million Dollar Difference

Jim McIngvale further proves that being different is better every day at Gallery Furniture in Houston, Texas. His furniture store grosses over one hundred million dollars a year, and curious retailers from all over the U.S. visit his store daily. Let me say that sales number again—one hundred million dollars—and that is only one store!

Started with just $5,000 and a pickup truck, Gallery Furniture opened for business in 1981. A college dropout, McIngvale always dreamed of starting his own business, but he didn't have much money. What he did have was guts. He and his wife Linda thought people moving to Houston to capitalize on the oil boom would need and buy furniture. But with little money it is hard to start any kind of business.

So Linda and Jim got up very early every Saturday and drove a rented truck five hours to Dallas and paid cash to purchase small amounts of furniture. They stayed overnight and returned early Sunday morning in time to open the store. Gradually, all of their hard work began to pay off. Then in late 1981 the economy in Texas collapsed when the oil market went farther south. The population of Houston dwindled as people left the area in search of jobs. It was certainly not a great place to be trying to sell furniture. But adversity is something some people thrive on, and Jim McIngvale is one of those. Rather than quit, which is what most people would have done, McIngvale pressed on. The next step he took was certainly different.

McIngvale took his last $10,000 and purchased some late-night advertising on TV. He decided to appeal to the long-term residents of Houston—he thought with their support his business could make it. But he did know he had to do something different; after all, this was his last $10,000 so it better work.

The television commercial featured him holding money and saying, with a cheesy smile on his face, "Gallery Furniture Saves You Money!" They were a big hit! Over a billion dollars in sales, and nineteen years later Gallery Furniture still uses the same simple but effective slogan.

Gallery Furniture is like no other retailer you'll ever see. The store is what retailers call a destination point, a place that is an experience. Some other stores have gone now to the concept I'm about to explain, but arguably nobody does it as well as Gallery Furniture.

The store has not just furniture but a bowling alley, a children's playground, a restaurant, and several celebrity displays—Shaquille O'Neal's shoes, Princess Diana's pearl necklace, and even $500,000 worth of Elvis Presley's possessions including his 1956 Lincoln Continental. The Elvis paraphernalia is likely one of the smartest investments the McIngvales have ever made, as the traffic and excitement to see the collection have resulted in millions of dollars' worth of business.

I love the McIngvales' philosophy. They combine crazy, creative promotions with sound business practices. Not only is Gallery Furniture a fun place to visit, it has great service. For example, the McIngvales will deliver your purchases the same day. If you're not happy, they will make things right immediately—no haggling or making you jump through hoops. They listen to their customers and react accordingly. In fact, visit Gallery Furniture, and you can find the man they call Mattress Mac walking the floor looking for more clues to success.

Jim and Linda McIngvale's Gallery Furniture is a terrific example for you to follow. Do things differently, perform in a way that is contrary to the norm and apply sound business practices, and your venture will work. Doing business differently is not only a very good philosophy in general, it is also fun.

Please, if you are contemplating opening any kind of retail establishment, visit Gallery Furniture in Houston, Texas (you can fly there inexpensively on Southwest Airlines) and bring your video camera. You'll learn so much (both on the plane and at the store) and be so motivated, you'll start to see your own dream take shape. You can also visit them on the Web at www.gallery.com.

How Can **You** Do This Now?

Okay. I've told you that one of the secrets to success in your own entrepreneurial endeavor will be to perform in a way that's contrary to the norm, or "be different." I told you of my friend Dan Kennedy who has written the book *How to Succeed in Business by Breaking All the Rules*. I talked to you about Krispy Kreme Doughnuts, a company that does something very simple very differently and very, very successfully. I've explained a few of the ways we do things differently at Grunder Landscaping Company. You're probably wondering how you can differentiate what you're doing from everyone else. Well, actually, it's quite easy.

Here's how to go about it—drum roll please! In every industry there are weaknesses that run rampant. Make those weaknesses your venture's strengths, and you can be successful.

Look at your particular industry and marketplace and analyze, think through, how the people in it go about things. This is simple, don't make it difficult. Now try as hard as you can to look at your endeavor from your *client's* point of view. Is what everyone does what they *should* be doing? Once you've figured out what the particular marketplace is lacking, what it does poorly, make that your strength. This will then become your competitive advantage.

A competitive advantage is the thing about your business that makes you better than everyone else. At Grunder Landscaping Company, it's our high standards. We feel that our standards and performance are higher than any other landscaper in our marketplace. Everything we do, we try to do the best way possible. Our whole team knows we cut no corners. What you want to do is to look for something in your business that you can be better at than everyone else and, at the same time, be different. It's a very effective way to work.

My friend Dave Tucker does this very well. His company produces CLIP software, used by thousands in the green industry. From user conferences to sponsoring chat rooms to giving great service, Dave's company identified all the sore points and needs in other green industry software companies and sought to be different by making other companies' weaknesses his company's strengths.

In my case, in the landscaping business, it's quite easy to be different just by operating in a way that most other corporations consider standard operating procedure. Let me give you an example.

In your life, admit it, when you've tried to get some type of contractor to come over to your house and do some work, it's been a struggle, correct? Let me guess. They didn't return your phone calls. They were late. They didn't deliver the job as promised. Some things went wrong, and they didn't bother to show up to try and work with you to make them right. Once they got the check, they were gone. Often you can't even get them out to your place to talk about what you'd like to have done in the first place. If you lived in Lexington, Kentucky and won the Kentucky Lottery on Saturday night, and called three contractors on Monday telling them that you just won the lottery, and you'd like to spend a million dollars around your home, would they come out and see you? It's likely that two of them would never call you back, and the third one would tell you he's coming over to meet with you and then never show up. Sure, I'm exaggerating a little for effect, but in general if you find a contractor who shows up when he says he's going to and makes things right that went wrong, you're probably looking at a very successful contractor.

Several years ago, on the other hand, when I was trying to get a newsletter together for my growing business, I called three ad agencies to see if I could talk with them about the possibility of them helping me with a newsletter. By the following morning at 10:00, all three of them had made a personal visit to me, all making a pitch for my business, making me feel that I was very important to them and that they would really like to do business with me.

That's what I'm talking about when I say that things in the contracting business considered contrary to the norm are actually standard operating procedures in most other businesses. Whether you're a contractor, the owner of an ad agency, have a small engine repair shop, or run a restaurant, you ought to be able to learn from this secret to success.

Back in my early days in the business, I looked around at all the landscapers in Dayton, Ohio, and those I read about in other towns in some of the magazines I read. And I concluded that, in general, many landscapers were terrific people who come over to your house and tell you what's wrong with your Norway spruce or your Dwarf Korean Lilac or your rosebushes. But many of them did not have strong abilities in the area of management and marketing. To this day, this is still a problem. Landscapers know a lot about the technical side of the business as far as what plants work where, how do you make sure plants survive and thrive, how do you install pavers patios, how do you prune, and so on. But a lot of them don't spend any time worrying about how they can manage, market, and motivate their company better. And those are the truly important elements of success. I call it the Three M Success Plan—management, marketing, and motivation. All three of those must be present to make a business work. It's just as important to success as the technical side of the business. All I heard from my friends' parents in the beginning was that "Landscapers are not reliable, they don't deliver as promised." After little more than three years in the business, I'd heard many times "You at age sixteen are more professional and reliable than most of the well-established landscapers in town."

I've made a small fortune in the landscaping business by basically delivering what we promised, paying attention to details, being polite, and following up to make sure our clients are happy. And by showing up for appointments on time.

A Lesson Learned the Hard Way

This practice (being on time) took a while to perfect. You might say I learned it the hard way. I had gotten a call inquiring about our services from an entrepreneur I'd read about many times in the local business paper. We were to meet at his office at 10:00 a.m. on a Thursday. I unfortunately (or fortunately is how I look at it today) showed up at 10:40 and never called the gentleman to tell him I was running late. I scurried up the steps, briefcase in hand, and told the receptionist I was there to see Mr. Williams. She said to have a seat. Two minutes later the receptionist returned and said, "Mr. Williams said you are forty minutes late, but he'll still see you. It will be a while. I'll come and get you when he's ready to see you."

Forty minutes later she took me back to see Mr. Williams. I felt like such a fool, "Why couldn't I have just been on time?" I thought. Mr. Williams introduced himself and his office was very impressive. The walls were full of small business awards and pictures of his family.

He then said, "Marty, you were forty minutes late, and you didn't even have the courtesy to call. You wasted my time and yours. That's why I made you wait on me. To be successful you must be on time for meetings. It is disrespectful not to be. Now, show me what you can do for my company."

I then proceeded to show him how we could make his building look great. To my amazement he bought the job. But only after I promised him to be on time from here on out. Sensing he had done a good deed and taught a young man a good lesson, he walked me to the lobby and told me I was a "heck of a salesman."

I skipped to my truck with my briefcase in hand. In that shiny, leather briefcase was a $10,000 contract. I put the briefcase on the ground and opened my truck door, got in, and backed up over my briefcase, squashing it in the process. Needless to say, I did not go back inside to ask for another contract. The one with the tire tracks would do just fine. I would, however, never forget the importance of being on time. Learn this lesson at a young age, and you will reap the benefits your entire life. To this day, we are known at Grunder Landscaping Company for being on time—something many contractors could do but don't.

To highlight and promote this attribute, I've taken it even a step further. Often I set an appointment with someone I'm trying to impress at an odd, specific time, like 10:27 a.m. Not 10:15, not 10:30, but 10:27. This really communicates my strength and completely differentiates me from all others. It gets me noticed and talked about. The local business paper even did a story on me and called me "the 10:27 landscaper."

Make Their Weakness Your Strength

If you are a stockbroker, why not get a pager, a cell phone, and an e-mail address, and make yourself accessible to your clients most of the time? Sure, you have to sleep, but poor communication is one of my biggest gripes with stockbrokers. Make it your strength, and you're different. You've seen the commercials for Etrade and Accutrade and all the others that portray the stereotypical stockbroker. Why not take the alternate approach and really take an interest in your clients? Do this and watch your business boom. If you own a restaurant, why not spend the time you need to train your employees to be as polite as possible and to say "thank you" to their clients? If you own an auto repair shop, what do you think your clients would think if the mechanic came out from the back, and delivered their car back to them in person, after wiping down the dashboard and cleaning the whole car up and washing it? And told Mr. or Mrs. Jones, who just picked up their repaired car, to call him personally if they had any problems, and then proceeded to give them his business card. Look for things in your business that will differentiate you from everyone else. Take some little extra steps to make your clients feel really welcome.

Service: One of the Best Strengths

My friend David Gutridge and his wife Marcia are two of the most energetic, enthusiastic, and positive people you'll ever meet. They are a model for others to follow. Their attitudes are contagious. I frequently have lunch with David. He is a brilliant businessman who has given me much sound advice. But no advice he's given me was more powerful than a story he shared with me.

David told me of his friend's mom who complained vigorously about the rude treatment she received at the grocery store. Frustrated, she told her son that "she would buy just about anything from anyone (if she needed the product or service) if they were nice to her." In other words, she didn't care as much about the price as she did about the service. David and I concluded that blustery winter day that his friend's mom had said something simple yet profound. Unfortunately (or fortunately for me as a business consultant), most businesses don't get this. They hire people on the spot without checking them out, offering them any training, or even sharing the company mission statement with them. Yet entrepreneurs grumble when they don't make money and blame their failure on other factors constantly, such as the economy, bad help, and difficult customers.

In the airline industry, there were two airlines that were profitable in 2000. One was Midwest, the other Southwest. The airlines are completely different companies with no connection. But they both offer great service. Is it any coincidence that both had the highest customer satisfaction rating? Should you be surprised to hear that? Not really.

You would think that other companies could try to follow their lead, but they don't. The secret of success in the airline industry is right there for them all to see, but they don't get it. It is obvious that consumers have gotten sick of poor service from the major airlines. The attention Southwest and Midwest give their clients is not just different but very profitable. The secret is here for you, too—be different. You can even go into a saturated market and still grab market share and excel by being different.

Don't Overlook the Obvious!

You don't necessarily have to think too hard. Many times it is the obvious that is overlooked and not done. Take what a thoroughbred horse trainer started doing several years ago.

D. Wayne Lucas is the most winning trainer of all time. He's won over 200 million dollars in purses. The way he did this was simple, yet different. He asked high net worth individuals if he "could train some horses for them" and even came right out and said, "Can I have your business?" Though this is done in many other businesses, in the horse training business, it wasn't done at the time.

Lucas' pitch was so different people noticed him. His potential clients were not accustomed to this, but they felt his enthusiasm and they believed in him. Consequently, they sent him many superb horses. But Lucas' "different" behavior didn't stop there. Once clients visited their prized possessions in a Lucas barn, they would never go anywhere else. Why? Again, Lucas did something simple and obvious yet very different. His barns were beautiful.

Horseracing is a nomadic profession. Horses are stalled at a racetrack for a period of one to four months, and then they move on. When D. Wayne Lucas moved in, he made certain his barns were immaculate. He laid new sod, planted flowers, hung flowering baskets, and polished everything. Rules for the help were posted as well as motivational sayings. All of Lucas' employees were neatly dressed and courteous, and his clients loved this. Horse owners who were used to dirty barns and not being treated like they were appreciated soon felt like kings. And they paid Lucas much more than others to receive this treatment.

Lucas' competition didn't like his antics and labeled him a "promoter," not a trainer! Funny thing about this, though—many trainers do now what he did then, and they too have been very successful following Lucas' "different" ways.

Words of Wisdom from a Grand Old Man

My attorney and friend is Hani Kallas. He was a childhood friend of my brother and was always fun to be around. Those of us who knew him as a boy always believed he'd be successful. And we were right.

Hani graduated from the University of Cincinnati Law School in 1994 (third in his class!) and went right down the street to work for Vorys, Sater, Seymour and Pease LLP. Vorys, Sater, Seymour and Pease is a prominent, very successful firm; in other words, not just your average law student gets a job there. Part of the orientation process at Vorys, Sater, Seymour and Pease is to sit down and talk with Jacob E. Davis or "Jake" as his associates call him.

Jake is a legend in Cincinnati. Born in Beaver, Ohio, in 1905, Jake became an attorney at age twenty-five. In the many years since then, he's served as a judge, congressman, special assistant to Secretary of the Navy Forrestal, and assistant general counsel of the Navy Department. He's also been a trustee of Ohio State University, and president of the Ohio State University alumni association. "He has an air about him you can't help but admire," said Hani.

That first week at Vorys, Sater, Seymour and Pease, Jake took Hani and another new, young attorney to lunch at the five-star Maisonette Restaurant. I've been there; it's a real ritzy place that the aristocrats of Cincinnati have been going to for decades. Hani had never been there before, so he was in awe of the surroundings as well as the great man he was with. At the end of the lunch, Jake

182

cleared his throat and was ready to give the young attorneys some advice.

Hani could feel it was going to be something that would guarantee his success as an attorney. Obviously, Jake Davis knew what it took to be successful. The two young attorneys sat motionless, ready to take in Jake's profound wisdom. "Young men," Jake said, "when a client calls you, call them back that day." Jake then paid the bill, and they went back to the office. To this day, Hani calls all of his clients back the same day. When I heard this story, it just further proved that little things make a big difference. Of all the things Jake Davis could have shared with Hani and the other new attorney, he shared something very simple. Some people might even consider it obvious.

reality check

Many times performing in a way that's contrary to the norm is so easy, you'll be amazed. Here are nine things you can do to stand out in the crowd: (1) Have your phones answered on or before the third ring by a smiling, live professional. No voice mails please. (2) Spend money to have your logo and image professionally done. (3) Make sure that all quotes, letters, and correspondence are professionally typed up. (4) Respond immediately to all inquiries. (5) Call all prospects back within two hours, clients within one hour. (6) Listen to your clients/prospects instead of talking. (7) Be honest—always, even if it costs you a sale. (8) Say "thank you for the opportunity" if you don't make the sale, and "thanks, you made my day" if you do make the sale. (9) Come right out and ask for the sale—few do it.

The problem is many businesses don't do this. America Online, for example, has one of the worst customer service departments I've ever run into. I've called General Motors to complain and gotten nowhere. I've wanted to spend money with countless firms only to have them **never** return my call. Bad service is everywhere. Conversely, I've grown Grunder Landscaping from zero to 2.5 million in ten years using Jake Davis' tip.

If You Need Any Further Convincing

This eighth secret to success should be so clear to you now that you can't wait to get started. But to drive home the point, call L. L. Bean at 1-800-221-4221 and order a new suitcase. When it arrives (overnight if you wish), pull it over to the legendary Nordstrom's Department Store and fill it with clothes. Oh, and don't worry, if you don't like those new shoes, Nordstrom's will take them back (even if you wore them), no questions asked. Go to the airport with your new suitcase and clothes and fly Southwest Airlines to Columbus, Ohio. Chances are you'll save a lot of money, and have fun on the way there listening to their employees say things like, "Weather at our destination is 50° with some broken clouds, but they'll try to have them fixed before we arrive. Thank you and remember nobody loves you or your money more than Southwest Airlines." And you'll arrive safely (they've *never* had a fatality). Once there, take a limo to a Hampton Inn. At Hampton you'll be greeted by an enthusiastic employee, the smell of freshly baked chocolate chip cookies, and the promise that if "you're not one hundred percent satisfied, you don't pay." Once in your clean, comfortable room, call me at 1-937-847-9944 and I'll come pick you up at 6:07 p.m. and drive you to J. Alexander's Restaurant for the best prime rib, salad, desserts, and service you'll find anywhere and give you a tour of Grunder Land-scaping Company, a national-award winning company offering uncompromising quality and unparalleled service.

If you do this experiment, you will return home with no doubt in your mind that to be successful in your entrepreneurial venture you **must** be different. Anyone can compete on price; it's the simplest of all strategies and also the most competitive. Nordstrom's, Southwest Airlines, L. L. Bean, BMW, Lexus, J. Alexander's Restaurant, Dr. Dan O'Brien (my dentist), Hampton Inns, Iams, and Grunder Landscaping Company, just to name a few, compete on something other than price. They compete by offering superior service and quality. Strangely, they also are the most successful too! Be different and be nice and watch your business become one others try to mimic. And don't worry, your competitors won't catch up too soon. Even though the concept is simple, people are afraid of the hard work it will take to make it work. And that leads to the last secret—The Harder You Work, the Luckier You Get.

chapter ten

The Harder You Work, the Luckier You Get

*"I am a great believer in luck.
The harder I work, the more I have of it."*

—Thomas Jefferson

O ne of my favorite actors is Joe Pesci. In *My Cousin Vinnie*, he plays an attorney trying to get his cousin "off" on murder charges. It is his first case and, although he makes his cousin very nervous, he eventually beats the rap, and his cousin is free to go. The movie is absolutely hilarious and certainly worth renting one night.

My Cousin Vinnie should prove to be an inspirational movie for you as well. Especially when you see what a gifted actor and comedian Joe Pesci is, and realize that, at one time, life wasn't so easy or funny for Joe Pesci. His story is a great example of what hard work can lead to. At the age of four, Joe's father, Angelo, enrolled him in acting classes, dance classes, and music classes. Angelo thought his perfect son could make it in show business, and so he pushed him to the limit. At the age of five, Joe was making regular appearances on the NBC TV variety show *Startime Kids*. As Joe grew up, however, things didn't progress like he thought they would. He did land a role in the 1975 movie *Death Collector*, but that was about it for Joe.

With no acting work, Joe had to take jobs as a hair stylist, construction worker, and letter carrier just to make ends meet. Things got so bad he even thought of abandoning his dream of making it to Hollywood. Then he went to work as a manager at a Bronx, New York, restaurant. But all the while Joe still kept his dream in the back of his mind, and he still practiced and thought about acting, taking time during his breaks and at home to stand in front of the mirror and reenact different movies. After all, the restaurant business, if you're really good at it, is entertainment in a sense. People pay to come see a performance: the waiters, the maitre'd, and the chef are the actors, and the restaurant and all of its trimmings, the stage set. So he wasn't entirely removed from being an actor as it was.

One day, an associate at the restaurant said Robert DeNiro had called for him. "Sure he did," Pesci mused to himself. If you are familiar with Pesci, can't you visualize him saying this? Even though he assumed it was a joke, he thought, "What the heck, I'll return the call and see who's trying to trick me." It *was* Robert DeNiro, and he wanted Pesci to play the role of boxer Jake LaMotta's brother Joey in the movie *Raging Bull*. DeNiro had heard of Pesci through an acquaintance and decided to pursue him personally. Pesci did great in the role, being nominated for an Oscar and later going on to win an Oscar for playing Tommy DeVito in *GoodFellas*.

Being Prepared—the First Step

Since Pesci was prepared when DeNiro called on him, he hit a home run. You, in your own life, never know when you might get a shot at realizing your dream, so be ready. Be like the pinch hitter who sits at the end of the bench during a baseball game, always holding a bat in his hand and taking practice swings in between innings, or the firefighter who sleeps at the station waiting for a call. It's important to prepare yourself and practice for what you want to achieve someday. Since I am still trying to grow my speaking career, for example, I practice constantly. I close my eyes, and imagine myself speaking to a sold-out crowd in a huge arena. I watch big-time speakers like Brian Tracy, Zig Ziglar, Peter Lowe, and Les Brown, and envision myself in their shoes, thinking that one day I'll get a chance to do the same. That's what you need to do. If you think positively and visualize yourself winning, you will. If you keep working hard, you can and will get lucky.

Lucille Ball had a great quote on this subject I'd like to share with you. She said, "Luck? I don't know anything about luck. I've never banked on it, and I'm afraid of people who do. Luck to me is something else. It is hard work and realizing what is opportunity and what isn't."

The Simple Secret of Success

Through the years, self-improvement gurus have developed many ways to become successful. Some sound fairly complicated, such as Steven Covey's *Seven Habits of Highly Effective People*, for example. This self-improvement system is used by hundreds of thousands throughout the United States and worldwide. There are countless other successful programs, like Tony Robbin's *Personal Power*. Suze Orman has her *Nine Steps to Financial Freedom* that has given millions of people a blueprint to follow for financial success. And then there are my own two favorite self-improvement gurus.

One is the late but great Earl Nightingale, who preached very simply, "You are and you become what you think about." The other simple philosopher, Brian Tracy, said, "If someone else has done it, that's all the proof that you need to tell yourself you can do it, too." Thanks, Brian. Because of you, I'm a successful speaker and author. Brian Tracy is my favorite motivator because of the great pains Brian takes to explain success in simple terms.

There are, however, people peddling all kinds of self-help contraband. There are promises to make money without working, to make money overnight (or in no time at all), or make money by spending tons of money on consultants. We even see people resort to crime in an attempt to be successful. In general, anything that sounds too good to be true is. Success, plain and simple, comes from working hard. And here is the ninth step to success, to your entrepreneurial success—the harder you work, the luckier you get. This was said by Thomas Jefferson and later by Samuel Goldwyn, a Polish-American movie producer. I am so convinced that it is true I dare you to show me an example of a successful person who doesn't work hard!

In 1951, a horrible film titled *Bedtime for Bonzo* was produced. The star was none other than Ronald Reagan, who was in his forties at the time. But this actor was no failure. Fifteen years later, Reagan became governor of California and twenty-nine years later, at age sixty-nine, he became President of the United States. Another "late in life" success story was Sam Walton, the founder of Wal-Mart. He didn't get Wal-Mart off the ground until he was forty-four. Sam Walton and Ronald Reagan both knew hard work opened doors to success. They never gave up and were such driven, positive-thinking people that what others might consider failure, they considered stepping stones to the future. You may think you could never do what Walton or Reagan did, but neither did they when they started out.

For every one successful pharmaceutical breakthrough, for instance, there are 5,000 failures. Drug companies like Merck and Pfizer spend billions each year on research and development looking for that one drug that will cure some disease or illness. We should all be thankful the entrepreneurs who started Merck and Pfizer and others weren't quitters. Their work has saved lives.

Orville and Wilbur Wright, likewise, worked countless hours in their bicycle shop in Dayton, Ohio, to perfect the first airplane.

Everywhere you look, someone is making it with hard work. Hard work can even make up for lack of talent and natural ability. My father spoke shortly before he died about how I was when I was young. Dad said I was always the first one up and out the door. He said I was really motivated to work hard. He seemed very proud of this trait in me, but I learned it from him. My dad did things he never should have done, like building our house, building a basketball pole and court, making me a trailer to haul my mowers on, and building a large horse-riding arena at age sixty-six all by himself! I will always work hard; it's a habit.

Since I started my business in 1983 at the age of fifteen until today, I have worked hard. Everybody can't graduate first in their class, and I realized early on I was never going to be the smartest one in class, but I could achieve a lot if I worked hard. So that's what I did.

Once I got going, I really became excited. Every day when I came home from school, I would quickly change out of my school uniform into my work clothes, go jump on my tractor, and drive six miles with brother Rich to mow lawns.

As I told you earlier, I graduated 153rd out of more than 300 in my high school class and was nearly thrown out of the University of Dayton for poor grades. Finally, I figured things out and graduated. I always tried hard, but things like chemistry, economics, and philosophy didn't come easy. Upon graduating, I applied what I learned at UD with a lot of hard work to create a multimillion-dollar-a-year operation. My speaking, writing, and consulting career is now taking off due to hard work as well. This can and will happen to you.

Take My Secret and Run with It!

I tell my audiences that I'm probably not any smarter than you, I'm certainly not any better looking than you, but what I may have on you at this point in your life, is that I've worked a lot harder than you. Now that you know my secret to success, take it and run with it. If you're in sales, don't go home when you think you're done. Push yourself. Stay for another half hour and make three more phone calls. Send out five more notes to prospective clients. Go to that personal development seminar on Saturday. Stay up late and read a book on a successful entrepreneur. Make one more appointment

"I HAVE ALWAYS ADMIRED ENTREPRENEURS BECAUSE THEY GIVE UP THEIR EIGHT-HOUR-A-DAY JOB TO WORK SIXTEEN HOURS!"

—Clay Mathile, entrepreneur and former owner of Iams

for Tuesday night. Do whatever it takes, and soon this hard work will begin to pay dividends. You see, the harder you work, the more opportunities you will run into. Soon one of these opportunities you're running into will catapult you to success.

Take marketing, for example. Spending big bucks is not necessary. Hard work is! Most people can't afford to market using vast

> "IF THE POWER TO DO HARD WORK
> IS NOT TALENT, IT IS THE BEST POSSIBLE
> SUBSTITUTE FOR IT."
>
> **—President James Garfield**

sums of money. Those who do spend big bucks are most likely either huge corporations with money to burn or lazy businesspeople who are afraid of hard work. The neat thing about cheap marketing is if it doesn't work, it's no big deal. You just learn from the situation and go on.

Hard work is unquestionably a key element in being a successful entrepreneur. Your success as an entrepreneur is decided mostly by your own effort. In many cases your income is directly related to the effort you put forth.

An interesting thing about hard workers is that they tend to overcome rejection and failure very quickly. Hard workers see failure and rejection as opportunities—opportunities to learn and do better the next time. Hard workers become so focused on the goals they're trying to achieve they ignore all the obstacles that are jumping out in front of them.

Once you succeed at an endeavor, your confidence will grow and grow and grow, and you will find it easy to work hard, and then harder. If you work hard enough and stick with it, almost any goal can be achieved. In 2000 we saw Lance Armstrong overcome cancer to win the Tour de France! This race is to bicycling what the Kentucky Derby is to horse racing, the Super Bowl to football, the World Series to baseball, and the Indianapolis 500 to auto racing. The fact that he won is a story, but the fact that he overcame testicular cancer to do it is both mind-boggling and inspirational. The story of Lance Armstrong is a clear example of what hard work can do. When Lance was diagnosed with cancer in Austin, Texas, he could have shriveled up and died, literally. But he wanted to live and put forth the effort to live and be a winner. Many think his goal of winning the Tour de France actually helped cure him of cancer. His hard work created luck. How lucky do you think you are? Start working hard, and you'll get lucky.

Many small companies can make it in the big arenas. The following children's toys and/or movies, for instance, have all been started by small firms: Barney, Cabbage Patch Kids, Beanie Babies, Teletubbies, Teenage Mutant Ninja Turtles, and Thomas the Tank Engine. Many times big companies are too slow and full of bureaucracy to react quickly to an opportunity. A little person comes up with an idea, and a year later they are a multimillionaire, all because they worked hard and ignored what the voices said. I could go on for hours giving you reason after reason and case after case, evidence that hard work creates luck.

A while ago, I read a story about Damon Bailey, the fabled basketball player from Heltonville, Indiana. Damon was recruited to play for coach Bob Knight at Indiana University while he was in the eighth grade. He eventually went on to play for Knight and is probably the most popular player ever to play basketball there, and he did this all with hard work. He says he learned what hard work would do for you from Bob Knight—"I saw how he took average kids and busted their rear ends to turn them into something special." Bailey's story is an example of what hard work can do. Hard work breeds success.

The One Talent We ALL Have

I want to end this book with the most important motivational and educational message I have for you.

There are people born with an unbelievable amount of physical talent. Some for sports like Michael Jordan, Ken Griffey, Jr., Tiger Woods, and Jaromir Jagr. Some for music such as Billy Gilman, Aretha Franklin, and Faith Hill. Still others for their looks such as Mel Gibson, Robert Redford, Marilyn Monroe, and Cindy Crawford. Then, there's you and I and everyone else. We all have one talent in common. Every single person has this, young and old. It is the ability to work hard. The challenge is to **use** this talent you have. And that's a big challenge. Most people are lazy (notice I said *most*). Most people aren't successful either. They're not successful because they never pursue their dreams; they just talk about them. They only pick a passion and stop there. They buy my book, read Chapter One and quit, saying "I'll finish it later" and never do. Successful people stay up late reading the entire book. They pick their passion, and get paid to learn more about it, honing skills they will use later. While getting paid to learn, they set goals and make targets to shoot for.

194

I see plenty of entrepreneurs who have the ability to be successful, but they aren't willing to work hard enough to get there. These "potential" entrepreneurs become frequent golf outing champs, Internet experts, and the number one selection on the speed dialers of those who are always looking to goof off. These same people, because of all the playing they do, are always behind, frequently feel overwhelmed, and often amazed at how other people get so much done.

I would love to take a day off each week to go to the racetrack early in the morning and watch the horses work out and get pampered. I could spend hours talking "horse" with other trainers and owners. But if I did this, I would never be able to run a very successful landscaping company, write books, produce a newsletter called *Winning Strategies*, advise other entrepreneurs on management, marketing, and motivation, speak all over the U.S. and Canada, and be home for dinner with my family at least two nights during the week and both nights on the weekend.

My long-range goal is that all my businesses will enable me to "retire" by the time I am forty-five and be able to spend more time with my kids, go to see the horses, and continue to help other entrepreneurs by speaking, teaching, and writing. But I have a lot more hard work to do before then!

I hope you can see how powerful hard work can be. Success is a process, not an event. You will make many mistakes in your journey to success. Your ability to overcome mistakes will be a big part of your realizing your dream. Mistakes force you to do it right the next time. Hard work enables you to overcome many inadequacies.

Will I Ever Be Able to Take It Easier?

It's important not to be confused by what I'm saying about hard work. In the early days of Grunder Landscaping Company, I worked eighty to ninety hours a week. I had to, to get to where I wanted to go. But I was single and didn't have children. Today, with a great family consisting of a wife and four kids, I cannot and do not want to work ninety-hour weeks. From time to time, my busy speaking and consulting practice forces me to do this, but it is rare.

Early on in your entrepreneurial endeavor and maybe for quite a while, you will have to work many long hours. So make certain as I said earlier in this book that your family knows and understands this. But at some point, it will get better. To get to the point where you are working only fifty to sixty hours per week, you must learn how to work. By that I mean you need to learn systems. Systems are routines that enable you to do a task easier and quicker. Systems as I said earlier in the book enable companies like McDonald's to achieve success. This is something that takes time to learn. In your role as the founder, CEO, president, entrepreneur, or whatever of your company, you are carrying out your plan or the first eight steps of this book. Step number nine is how it all comes together.

Hard Work Doesn't Just Mean Drudge Work!

I have worked with or visited more than two hundred landscape contractors in the past several years, and the most successful ones know how important it is to work *on* your business and not just *in* your business. I have a client in Florida who has a $600,000 a year highly profitable organization, and he doesn't do anything but work

196

reality check

Before I close here, let me remind you that when you do become a successful entrepreneur, don't forget to thank those (family, clients, and team members) who have gotten you to where you are today. As coach Bear Bryant would ask his freshmen football players every fall, "Have you called your folks yet to thank them?" Most of the players would look at him in confusion or amazement as to why a rough and tough football coach would ask such a caring question. Bryant would go on to explain: "No one ever got to this level without the help of others. Call your folks. Thank them." No one gets to any pinnacle of life without the help of others—no one!

on strategy, leading, motivating, and controlling. He sells a little, but he knows that his leadership is the most important thing he has to offer, and it is what brings his company the most money.

One of the best things a CEO can do is get caught looking out the window staring into space thinking—thinking about where he wants to be and how he's going to get there. That's exactly what I'm doing today, staring out the window, thinking tomorrow, next year, five years from now, and about how I'm going get to where I want to be in that time frame.

Successful entrepreneurs know how to lead, handle, and motivate people. You should be going to every seminar you can on these subjects, reading books like *How to Win Friends and Influence People*, *1001 Ways to Reward Your Employees*, anything on Jack Welch, *Winning Strategies* newsletter (available by calling 937-

847-9944) and finding other mentors who are excellent managers and leaders who can coach you to success.

The funny thing is that even though this seems so simple, it is rarely done. Why? Laziness? Maybe ... but more likely it is probably because people find themselves so busy planting, mowing, spraying, and fighting fires, they think they don't have time to work on this stuff.

I could write for hours on what a president or CEO should be doing ... and maybe I will, at a later date.

You're Successful!

You did it! You read the whole book. Congratulations and thank you. Congratulations for sticking with it and finishing, and thank you for reading it. I'm elated that my book is not going to be part of the eighty-three percent of books that reportedly don't get read. But don't get too comfortable; you have a long way to go, and I want to help you realize your dream. In the back of this book, you'll find a consultation coupon. Use this coupon to fax your question, idea, problem, goal, or whatever with it to my office at 937-847-8067. I will personally look at whatever you send (as long as it's in writing) and tell you what I think. On one of the final pages is also a coupon for a complimentary issue of *Winning Strategies*, my bimonthly newsletter designed to help with the management, marketing, and motivation of your entrepreneurial venture.

I travel all over the U.S. and Canada speaking on different topics, and I also help small business owners and aspiring entrepreneurs with a variety of small business issues. I would welcome an opportunity to work with your group.

Oh, yeah, if at any time during your entrepreneurial venture you feel like quitting, call me at 937-847-9944 and tell my office you're going to quit. They'll put you right through, and I'll give you a five-minute pep talk that will put you back on track. Best of luck—now get to work!

Receive a free critique from Marty Grunder

Please submit any question, idea, problem, or plan in writing, or any single printed piece—brochure, catalog, direct-mail package, advertisement, or the like—by mail or fax for a critique by Marty Grunder.

PLEASE SEND THIS COUPON
WITH YOUR MATERIALS TO THE ADDRESS BELOW.

Name: _____

Company: _____

Address: _____

City, State, ZIP: _____

E-mail address: _____

Phone: _____

Fax: _____

TERMS AND CONDITIONS:

No expiration date. Allow 2 to 4 weeks for return of submitted materials with Marty Grunder's comments and suggestions. This offer is available by mail or fax only. You may also need to contact your attorney or accountant for applicable regulations in your area. Only one coupon per person, please.

PLEASE BE ADVISED THAT ANY MATERIALS SUBMITTED TO MARTY GRUNDER! INC. MAY BE PUBLISHED AS EXAMPLES IN ANY OF MARTY GRUNDER'S AUTHORIZED PUBLICATIONS. DO NOT SUBMIT CONFIDENTIAL MATERIALS.

9770 Byers Road, Miamisburg, Ohio 45342
Phone: 937.847.9944 • Fax: 937.847.8067
The Harder You Work, The Luckier You Get

Book Ordering Information

Please send me _____ copies of Marty's book *The Nine Super Simple Steps to Entrepreneurial Success* for only $23.90 per copy (U.S. funds)—$18.95 plus $4.95 for shipping and handling.

Name: _____

Company: _____

Address: _____

City, State, ZIP: _____

E-mail address: _____

Phone: _____

PAYMENT INFORMATION:

Total: _____

_____ Check/Money Order (Make check payable to: Marty Grunder! Inc.)

_____ Credit Card: MasterCard, VISA, Discover

Credit Card No. _____

Expiration Date: _____

Cardholder Signature:_____

_____ I would like you to autograph the book.

_____ This is a gift for_____

Please sign it for them.

ORDER ONLINE AT WWW.MARTYGRUNDER.COM

9770 Byers Road, Miamisburg, Ohio 45342
Phone: 937.847.9944 • Fax: 937.847.8067
The Harder You Work, The Luckier You Get

Receive a free copy of the
Winning Stratgies Newsletter

What is *Winning Strategies*? *Winning Strategies* is a mini-seminar that arrives in your mailbox every other month. It will teach and inspire you to become a better manager, marketer, motivator, and person. Winning Strategies is jam-packed with marketing, management, and motivational ideas. Subscribers to the newsletter will also receive special offers and discounts.

YOU CAN ALSO ORDER ONLINE AT
WWW.MARTYGRUNDER.COM

Name: _____

Company: _____

Address: _____

City, State, ZIP: _____

E-mail address: _____

Phone: _____

Marty Grunder! Inc., 9770 Byers Road,
Miamisburg, Ohio 45342
Phone: 937.847.9944 • Fax: 937.847.8067
The Harder You Work, The Luckier You Get

More

great books

you *need* to **succeed!**

Jump Start Your Business Brain

Here are the facts: Most business owners have a higher probability of success playing a Las Vegas Slot Machine (32% odds) than investing in the average new product, service or advertising effort (10 to 25% odds). Now here's the good news: Doug Hall is on a personal quest to help you TILT THE ODDS IN YOUR FAVOR. Here, for the first time in print, he reveals the data-based wisdom, advanced technology and no-fail practical tactics that can make your business more innovative and more profitable. This national bestseller is the book you need to immediately start increasing your odds of business success with new products, services, sales and advertising efforts.

ISBN 1-55870-642-9, paperback, 256 pages, #70590-k

Export Import
Third Edition

You hear a lot about the global marketplace. But how much of the profit from the global economy is flowing to your company? None? Not enough? Then initiate or increase your across-the-borders business. Veteran exporter and importer Joseph A. Zodl makes getting started easy. He shows how you can guide your company into international trade—and minimize complications.

ISBN 1-55870-615-1, paperback, 160 pages, #70558-k

Novel & Short Story Writer's Market

Unique because of its focus on fiction markets—and fiction markets *only*—you're guaranteed to get more of the listings you really want, without hundreds of entries you don't need. From literary magazines and publishing houses to zines and online opportunities, this comprehensive volume provides easy-to-follow guidelines for submitting your work to more than 1,900 markets, with completely updated information on pay rates, e-mails, phone numbers and more.

ISBN 1-58297-147-1, paperback, 682 pages, #10812-k

Poet's Market

Get your poetry into print with *2003 Poet's Market!* It provides listings for more than 1,800 opportunities, including book publishers, small presses and journals, magazines, and chapbook publishers. Each entry includes contact information, types of poetry accepted, submission details, phone numbers, addresses, Web sites, emails and more. Special icons and indexes direct you to the markets you want FAST.

ISBN 1-58297-124-2, paperback, 572 pages, #10790-k

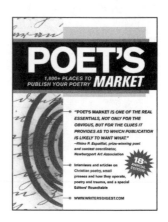

Guide to Literary Agents

Getting published depends on tenacity, skill and—often—having someone working for you who knows editors and producers on a first-name basis. Increase your odds of success by getting an agent—one that's right for you *and* your work. This book provides the names, mailing addresses, phone numbers, and e-mail addresses for more than 600 literary agents. Crucial to getting your fiction, nonfiction or screenplay into the hands of editors, publishers and filmmakers, these agents can help make your dreams come true!

ISBN 1-58297-146-3, paperback, 400 pages, #10811-k

Songwriter's Market

Get your songs published, recorded, and played on the air! There's no better resource for songwriters than this book. Updated every single year, it provides all the information you need to make contact with the music industry movers-and-shakers that can make your career. Inside you'll find more than 1,200 listings for every kind of music, including rock, hip-hop, classical, and country—even toe-tapping gospel.

ISBN 1-58297-123-4, paperback, 518 pages, #10789-k

Artist's & Graphic Designer's Market

This book is the key to getting your work sold, commissioned, published and shown. It's the most up-to-date resource available for ensuring that every contact you make is right for you and your work. With more than 2,500 market listings and industry contacts at your fingertips, *2003 Artist's & Designer's Market* provides all the information you need to score with ad and design agencies, magazine and book publishers, greeting card companies, art galleries, record labels, poster and print companies, syndicates and cartoon features.

ISBN 1-58297-122-6, paperback, 682 pages, #10788-k

Photographer's Market

You have photos to sell and *2003 Photographer's Market* has the buyers who want them. Inside you'll find more than 2,000 completely updated market listings with contact information for magazines, stock agencies, advertising firms, book publishers, greeting card and poster markets, newspapers, businesses, galleries and more, including 450 all-new listings.

ISBN 1-58297-121-8, paperback, 636 pages, #10787-k

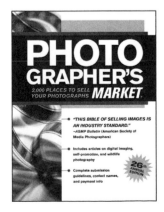

Writer's Market

Writer's Market is the world's #1 resource, helping countless writers get published and get paid. Inside you'll find the crucial information needed to contact more than 8,000 editors with specs on exactly what they're looking for, how much they pay, response times, and more. From book publishers and script buyers to consumer and trade magazines, there are thousands of valuable markets no matter what you write.

ISBN 1-58297-120-X, paperback, 1112 pages, #10786-k

Children's Writer's & Illustrator's Market

This essential directory brings together the two key aspects of children's publishing - writing and illustration. In one handy volume, you'll find helpful articles on how to make it in this rewarding field, plus detailed market information for more than 800 editors and art directors looking for work like yours!

ISBN 1-58297-148-X, paperback, 400 pages, #10813-k

Writer's Market Online

Get the most current market information today-delivered online! Writer's Market Online provides all the benefits of a Writer's Market-plus FREE access to WritersMarket.com. This extraordinary Web site offers all of the markets found inside, plus hundreds of additional listings, including two exclusive new sections: newspapers and online publications. And here's the best part: the editors of Writer's Market Online update and revise those entries with new, up-to-the-minute information every day!

ISBN 1-58297-125-0, paperback, 1112 pages, #10791-k